How to Explain

by

Louise Krug

Finishing Line Press
Georgetown, Kentucky

How to Explain

Copyright © 2024 by Louise Krug
ISBN 979-8-88838-751-1 First Edition
All rights reserved under International and Pan-American Copyright Conventions. No part of this book may be reproduced in any manner whatsoever without written permission from the publisher, except in the case of brief quotations embodied in critical articles and reviews.

Previously published:

"How to Hear What We Said" was previously published as "That's What We Said" in *Reed Magazine,* Fall 2019.
"How to be a Passenger" was originally published as "The Passenger" in *Juked*, Fall 2019.
"How to Be a Midwesterner in Three Acts" was published in *Essay Daily* on March 11, 2021.
"How to Have Double Vision" was previously published in *Sou'wester,* Spring 2021.
"How to Get Lost" was previously published in *eMerge,* Summer 2023.
"A List of What I Did and Did Not Know About Facial Paralysis" was previously published in *The Examined Life,* December 2023.

Publisher: Leah Huete de Maines
Editor: Christen Kincaid
Cover Art: Nick Krug
Author Photo: Nick Krug
Cover Design: Elizabeth Maines McCleavy

Order online: www.finishinglinepress.com
also available on amazon.com

Author inquiries and mail orders:
Finishing Line Press
PO Box 1626
Georgetown, Kentucky 40324
USA

Table of Contents

How to Explain 2

My Special Place on the Map 7

How to Get Lost 10

How Marriage is a Bank Account 14

How to Talk About God With A Personal Trainer 23

How to Dance 27

How to Find a Chiro 31

How to Make a Praise Sandwich 36

How to Quit 39

How to Be a Passenger 43

How to Look 47

How Not to Volunteer 51

How to Have Double Vision 54

How I'm Learning to Accept Myself as a Frequent Faller 57

How to Be a Midwesterner in Three Acts 60

How to Be a Legend: Filling Out My Daughter's Fourth-Grade Study Guide 64

A List of What I Did and Did Not Know About Facial Paralysis 69

To Olive and Bruce

Now

    Your new therapist asks you to do impossible tasks. Like a photo shoot with you smiling your half smile, a few teeth showing, the one you cover with your hands when you laugh. The one with half of your face working, and the other sagging silently.

    In the beginning, 17 years ago, there were high hopes that movement would come back. The facial nerves would regenerate, connect, and bring that half to life that had been dead since the brain surgery that had to go deep to remove a burst blood vessel. The most heartbreaking part is that you hoped for so long. You still hope, still feel movement, flutters around your lips, top and bottom. Nothing noticeable has ever happened, though.

    "Can Nick be in the picture?" you ask your therapist, sniffling. Blowing your nose. Dabbing your carefully-applied makeup from your eyes. Taking your glasses off, there to hide your bad eye as much as for vision purposes, cleaning them, and putting them on again. You repeat this routine about twenty times during your session.

    "Why not you alone? You could put up the photo in your house—frame it!—to show your kids how proud you are of how you look," she says.

    Over your dead body.

    She means well, this therapist, you remind yourself. You met her through a recommendation of one of your friends, and she was actually taking new patients, which is rare. Today she wears athleisure, purple patterned leggings and a tunic. She attends a Jazzercise class after your session every Friday.

    "What are you thinking?" she asks. "Don't tell me what you think I want to hear. Tell me the truth."

    Immediately, you say, "This will never work. Nothing will ever work. I will feel like this forever."

How to Explain

A neighbor girl comes over to our house sometimes and is my daughter's age, 10. She is polite and funny and unflinchingly honest, saying things to Nick like, "You may be 40 but you look older," and lets me know that all our snacks are stale. She always gives me her plate or cup when finished, when all the other neighborhood kids (and my own) just leave their dishes on the table. Disarming. Greeting her at the back door one afternoon, she asks me about my left eye, which looks different from my right in that it doesn't move much, and the lid is a little droopy.

"Why is your eye like that?" she says, looking up at me from the stoop on our back door, her black bangs plastered to her head, as it's a hot summer day in Kansas, a long braid down her back.

While I am thinking, she steps into our kitchen. My kids are swinging their legs at the table, licking popsicles, and I get her one, too. They are the red, white, and blue kind: Firecracker. Though my kids look nonplussed, they are probably listening to see what I say.

I launch into my three-sentence explanation: "Kind of like a stroke... Brain surgery...damage..." and she seems satisfied, if bored. I turn towards the dishes. That is the end of that. But not. Couldn't this interaction be better somehow? I am left feeling naked for the rest of the day. What if there was a completely different explanation? What if I lost it in a battle, and it was replaced with a magical one like Mad Eye Moody in *Harry Potter*? What if it hinted at a dangerous past, like Steve "Patch" Johnson in *Days of Our Lives*? What if, like Odin, a god in Norse mythology, I sacrificed my eye but gained a more sacred, divine level of wisdom in return?

What if, like the male model in the Hathaway Shirt advertisements of the 1950s, I just used my eye for added mystery? I read an article about the ad campaign's origins. With the eye patch, the model had what the director at the time called "story appeal," arousing reader curiosity. Without the ads, the man was just another man wearing a nice white shirt.

I would like to be just a person wearing a nice white shirt. I don't need story appeal, or powers.

*

I've worn an eye patch at two different points in my life. At age 9, an eye patch was a temporary way to stop my mysterious double vision while the doctors figured out what was wrong. I'd been having headaches and balance problems, too. When I was 22 and wearing an eye patch in the months before the surgeries, my grandmother ordered patches for me in pink, blue, and beige off the internet. A few weeks before my brain surgeries she had a St. Patrick's Day party. I helped serve Irish coffee and pound cake to twenty elderly women in hats. Grammy gave me a plastic green bowler hat "to get in the spirit." My boyfriend at the time called me Captain Hook, trying to be funny. I hated it.

I don't wear an eye patch anymore, mostly because 1. They're uncomfortable. Your skin inside the patch sweats, and the band messes up your hair. 2. I don't need to cover my "bad" eye anymore. By now my brain has gotten used to seeing double.

*

On a website "TV Tropes," one trope is The Eye Patch of Power, which falls under the grouping of Disability Superpowers like Genius Cripple, Handicapped Badass, and Super Wheel Chair.

Terry Taggart, played by Bette Davis in *The Anniversary*: described as "emasculating," "domineering," "evil," "manipulative," and "vindictive."

Eye Grafx, a website of over 20,000 combinations of eye patches, includes ones in leather, with "bling," for pets, and of "formal" style, covered in satin or lace.

On one website the eye patch is identified as a "Stock Costume Trait"

*

If you search "Long John Silver," what comes up first is "Long John Silver's," the fast-food fish restaurant. Its slogan is, "Fish Yeah!" and the logo is a cartoonish drawing of a pirate with an eye patch and also a peg leg and a parrot.

Next on the screen is the Wikipedia definition of Long John Silver, the character in *Treasure Island*, which is what I want. I discover he didn't even have an eye patch in the original book and illustrations done by Robert Louis Stevenson in 1881. A parrot and a peg leg, yes.

This keeps happening, thinking famous pirates have eye patches when they don't—Captain Hook didn't either, I find. Gold earrings, a hook for a hand, dark curly wig and a three-corner hat, yes. Eye patch, no. There are lots of theories as to why pirates are stereotyped to have eye patches, the most popular one seeming to be quite far-fetched for the time period (mostly 17th century, a time when people went from cradle to grave without bathing or brushing their teeth, but whatever) something about how eye patches helped pirates' eyes adjust quickly to the darkness of "below-deck." Seems murky at best. I buy the "story appeal" theory more.

*

J, a friend of my son's, is over at our house. J, 6, is full of questions: "Why are your stairs so creaky?" "Where is your cat?" "Why is your cat hiding?" and finally "What's wrong with your eye?"

Both of his parents are doctors, so I give a bit more advanced explanation, four sentences instead of three. J's parents are strict: there is a list of tasks they have to complete before they play video games: math problems, spelling words, musical instrument practice (J plays drums, his older brother guitar). He will understand more, I think. So I add words like "Cavernous angioma" and "hematoma," which are mistakes. "What?" he says. Then, "Oh. O.K." and he scampers off with my son to line up Minecraft figurines on the table and knock them down again.

It's not just kids who ask. Just the other day, a woman who I've been friends with for more than a year asked why I wore tape on my sunglasses. We were outside on our neighborhood sidewalk, having ran into each other when we were both on walks. It was a bright day, and I took my earbuds out.

"Is that a piece of tape?" she said.

It always takes me a minute to realize that someone is asking me about my appearance. When I see someone I know, I forget how I look.

I gave my five-sentence speech, using words like "depth perception" and "easier" and "balance." She seemed satisfied, saying goodbye quickly.

Who knows?

*

From *Treasure Island,* this is our first time seeing Long John Silver: "His left leg was cut off close by the hip, and under the left shoulder he carried a crutch, which he managed with wonderful dexterity, hopping about upon it like a bird. He was very tall and strong, with a face as big as a ham—plain and pale, but intelligent and smiling. Indeed he seemed in the most cheerful spirits, whistling as he moved about among the tables, with a merry word or a slap on the shoulder for the more favored of his guests."

From real life, a description of me in my own words: "Her left eye seemed to have a mind of its own, staying still when her right one looked toward something. She managed her sight reduction well, sometimes bumping into things but mostly using her hands to help her. She was tall and somewhat strong, with a sweatshirt on that said "Mrs. Claws" and black leggings. She was in cheerful spirits as well, bumping around her tiny kitchen, peeping under the Air Fryer lid and texting memes to friends."

I learned that in *Treasure Island*, we think Long John Silver is good but he turns bad mid-story. It seems he wants the treasure for himself and has been scheming all along. That seems to be a common thing with villains—either the audience knows they're bad right away, or it comes as a surprise once we've befriended them in our minds. I wish it could be the first way all the time in real life. An eye patch is an easy tell, too, so why not give every shithead in the world one?

Giving characters "story appeal" items such as eye patches is lazy, I think. Unrealistic. I never know when people are going to catch me unawares and remind me who they think I am. I have a "stock costume trait," but most don't. There's really no getting around that. But what to do with no one wanting to hear the explanation of the eye or the tape? Not really, it doesn't seem like. The questioning is never a conversation starter, only an ender. Sometimes, maybe an explanation is all they want.

Now

Yes, she means well, your therapist. But does that matter? During your first session, she asked you if you had three wishes, what would they be. You were at a loss, and shrugged your shoulders.

But now you know. You wish for peace in your own head. That's all.

Maybe meaning well just makes everything worse. When someone means well, you have to be nice to them, even if their idea is shitty, as opposed to someone who doesn't mean well.

Your therapist has lots of ideas she throws at you, all of which you hate. "When someone seems distracted by your face or can't look you in the eye, why not give them a boilerplate explanation?" she says. "Just tell them, with a few talking points, about the brain surgery and paralysis, to get it out of the way? Most of the time, people are just curious."

"But what if I don't want to?" you say. "I don't want to explain myself to people all the time."

"I get that," she says. But offers no antidote.

My Special Place on the Map: Filling Out My Son's School Project

Here is how I find my special place on the map. First, I look at the map of my country and find my state. I live in:

Compare Kansas, where you live now, to Michigan, where you grew up; it never gets old, though it probably should. Weigh flowering trees, dirt (black and clay-like here vs. sandy there) and beauty trends (in West Michigan, a highly Dutch-area, all the girls seemed to be tall, tan, and blonde, so tanning salons were something you all frequented from age 13 up, although that could have been the 1980's and 90's, too. And what are beauty trends in Kansas? The same??). "The squirrels are *black* up here!" is the one thing you remember about bringing a college boyfriend home for Thanksgiving. Be a snob about Kansas foods (Chicken and Noodles: what a starch-filled salt-lick!) and lack of knowledge about what a real lake looks like ("You shouldn't be able to see the other side!") but know in your heart that you can't imagine not living here. It's been so long. You think the Flint Hills are heart-stopping. Your children have Kansas on their birth certificates.

Then, I look at the map of my state and find my town. I live in:

When you get your first real job at thirty-four, move to a small city that has a downtown that is busy with important government workers during the week, but vacant on the weekends. Topeka is to Kansas what Kansas is to the rest of the country. Be strangely at peace with that. Coming from a hipster college town that is the bluest county in the state, you think it will be hard to get used to this place, but it isn't. Make friends with lots of neighbors like you have always wanted to, borrowing sugar and cackling about politics. Treasure the fact that your kids are still young enough to like their hometown, and know that will end soon. Hate anybody who makes fun of this place.

Next, I look at the map of my town and find my street. My street name is:

Run for block captain of your neighborhood. Uncontested. The former block captain, a man who had lived in the neighborhood forever, a hippie with a hot tub you envy, begged you to take over for him. Being block captain is more and less work than you imagined, and you are terrible at it (never emailing back other neighborhood officials, forgetting to bring new neighbors Welcome Baskets, skipping meetings, etc.).

And on my street, I find my house. My house number is:

Buy a house in which the yard is completely overgrown. The previous owner was a lawyer and told your realtor, "I'm from Oregon, so I like that woodsy feeling." Watch as your husband and family members remove the overgrowth for days, and say, "Don't get rid of that Secret Garden look!" The house was built in 1907, and the first night in the house you notice the stairs are so creaky that you tell your husband you've made a mistake. At least you can always hear your kids coming down after you've put them to bed.

Listen to cicadas, fireworks, the train, and the highway. Start applying under-eye concealer. Realize one night that your daughter insists on a shut-door policy for changing clothes. When did that happen?

In my house, I find my room. And in my room, I find me!

Break the rule about using your bed only for sleeping and not reading. Your side of the bed has three more blankets than Nick's. Lay your workout clothes out the night before, and stop folding your clothes, just shove them in drawers. You have bigger fish to fry. You are very close to forty.

Now

"What about a photography project where you take pictures of all sorts of asymmetrical objects found in nature? Like trees, flowers, or mushrooms. Everything is a little asymmetrical, and that can be beautiful!" she says.
    I just cry harder.

How to Get Lost

1. Nick, the kids, and I were invited to a birthday party for the father of my daughter's friend. They lived far out in the country on a ranch, in an old stone house. We wanted to go because they are nice people, but Nick was out of town so I had to drive. This was a problem, but could be overcome, if we planned carefully (I don't drive on the highway).

After breakfast, Nick and I peered at our phones, looking at the different routes. There were several, both of which followed roads I'd never heard of.

2. One evening, I was at a fundraiser in my neighborhood for the state book festival, and read a short essay I'd written on having double vision. Unusually, I was nervous, shaking in my legs, and my face was hot. Maybe it's because I knew most of the people in the audience, but I could barely look up from my paper. Afterwards, as I tried to leave the crowded room, people pressing into each other to try a bit of cheeseball or a lava cake, a man cornered me.

"I was at a dinner party and met your aunt," he said. He was much taller than me, and a close talker. "She told the whole table your story, and said that you had had a handsome French boyfriend. Boy, she sure likes to talk."

1. Together, a few days before the birthday party, Nick and I drove two of the routes that Siri gave us, one of which was extra-confusing because it involved a winding unmarked road, Ys that were tricky to remember which way to take, and blinking yellow lights.

2. By "my story," the neighbor man meant my brain surgeries and heartbreak when my then-boyfriend left me in the middle of that mess. I rarely think about that time because it is sad, and I've never really gotten over it.

A couple of days after the fundraiser, I dragged a dining room chair over to our high bookshelves. The old photo album was up there with photos of my French boyfriend and me, some of them only days before my headaches and tingling limbs, my E.R. visits, all of which would lead, months later, to the brain surgeries. In one photo, we are at a wax museum in Las Vegas, shaking our fingers at George W. Bush. I wore a tiny white t-shirt and denim miniskirt. I was 22. Blonde. Pretty. In another, he gazes out at the beach we lived by in Santa Barbara.

My kids are outside and Nick is working, so I let myself cry. I can't stop, and in intervals, the crying goes on for days, mostly when I am driving or on walks.

I start to worry.

1. On the day of the birthday party, the kids and I left our house an hour early for a thirty-minute journey. I drove like a cautious snail. We had a case of grape soda in our trunk, which was what I told the mom we would bring. It was a sunny day, and rural Kansas looked beautiful, the fields burned black like farmers do at that time of year to allow new growth. The sky was pure. The kids and I looked for, and found, the landmarks that told us where to turn or when to keep straight on the particular route I had chosen. Signs that only we would know: that gravel road, the Disney House, the log cabin. Finally, we found the house. But there was no one home. "Hi! We are here. Are we early?" I texted the mom. No reply.

2. I looked at my French boyfriend's Facebook account. He had "friended" me a few years back, a surprise, but we had never directly communicated. I surmised he had split from his model-esque Turkish wife by the drop-off of photos of her after 2016 and his "single" current status. I was happy about that. For the first time ever, I thought about emailing him. What I would say, what I would ask ("I am not the same person I was back then. How do you spend your time?"), but I couldn't tell if I really wanted to know information or was just curious to see what would happen. Did I want to forge a crack in my life? Would it be a crack? I was shocked that I could even think these thoughts.

1. Outside the empty stone house, I thought to check my calendar. The party was tomorrow. I harangued the kids back in the car. The trip home was a mess. I got turned around, and couldn't find that one gravel road. We ended up on a fast and busy two-lane where a truck laid on his horn at my slow speed. Everyone cried.

2. Things I had tried to reassure myself with to stop from crying:
a. You just want your youth back
b. You are in a better place now
c. Think of how wonderful your family is
d. Etc.
Nothing worked.

2. The next day we did the drive all over again, and found their house without a hitch. The party had BBQ, horseshoes, and a fishing pond, but we hadn't known so hadn't brought rods (not that we owned any). So we watched other people cast and reel. The rest of the guests seemed like family members, and there were no other kids. My daughter's friend seemed more interested in

lugging her baby cousin around than playing with her, so the kids and I played corn hole.

1. On the phone, I told my mom about the man's comment at the fundraiser. "Oh honey, I'm sorry. People can say such insensitive things." We start going down the road of how people are gossiping fools, but that's not what really bothers me. What I can't articulate to her at the time is a question: "When will I stop getting sad when I think about that time in my life?"

2. I email the French boyfriend. From what else I surmise on the internet, he has a young son and lives in Paris. My email is short, friendly but not inappropriate ("I just wanted to reach out and say hello…") and I send it after proofreading it once.

1. On the drive home, we stopped and got grocery store sushi as a treat. We also get Starbucks, which is in the grocery store, too. The kids get fruity drinks and I get a coffee at 4 p.m., guaranteed to hurt my sleeping chances. I don't care, I am just glad to be back to where the speed limit is 40. None of us reflects on the birthday party at all. It's like it never happened.

2. The French boyfriend writes back, and his email is equally benign. ("What a surprise to hear from you. Your email put a smile on my face….") After reading it, I feel deflated. What did I think would happen? Isn't this the best-case scenario? What was I wanting?
The night before, when I told Nick about sending it, he'd paused and said, "O.K., I trust you."

One night a few days later, Nick and I laid on our bed and I told him about the emails. I told him about the crying and the memories, Facebook, and my old photo albums, the like and the apology. The word "peace." I was nervous, because pain from the past is one thing, but emailing is another. Bringing exes into the present is something we have never done, not at all. I was pretty sure that Nick knew why I had done what I did, but there's always that tiny bit of doubt that maybe he didn't. Maybe he didn't understand me.

Nick stayed silent, and then he said again, "It's O.K., I trust you," and I knew that was true. Then he said, "Do what you have to do," and I did. I let things be.

Now

The question I can't get over is: how could I have been fine for so long after the brain surgery and now, 17 years later, feel awful again? Like my life falling apart was just yesterday? I met someone, fell in love, got married and had two children, went to graduate school and got a job, but it's like none of that ever happened.

How Marriage is a Bank Account

Checking Account: One week in November, 2021	Recent Transactions
Dillons #0088 Topeka, KS	-$2.17 2% milk, which the cashier forgot to ring up with everything else.
Dillons #0089 Topeka, KS	-$128.46 Panic buying. The pandemic is out of control, schools are closing again. I buy a 22-lb. turkey for a Thanksgiving dinner for just the four of us. I buy snacks for the kids I've never bought before: tiny boxes of raisins, orange creamsicles. Things for Nick and me: lots of coffee. Swedish fish. Stinky cheese.
Nick's Shower Maintenance #44 Topeka, KS	One softball-size knot of hair pulled from the shower drain. Update: Nick says it looked like a bulbous, hairy rat, not a softball, and it smelled worse than it looked.
AMZN Marketplace AMZN.COM/Seattle, WA	-$6.37 More battery-operated twinkly lights for decorating the house. I wound the strands around the stairway railing, along with some red tinsel. It took me a long time to get it right. Like multiple do-overs of unwinding everything. Bruce helped by tangling the strands. When Nick came home from shooting a wedding, he helped by critiquing my aesthetic. But then he really did help with some master-rigging.

Nick's Trampoline Park #88	Despite the cold, most days the kids are willing to play with Nick on the trampoline for about 25 minutes while I play with my phone/get dinner ready. He has invented a game called, "Smash Ball," which involves him tagging the kids with a halfway-aired beach ball. Today, I sit inside and drink tea while looking at a Lands End catalogue. It is heavenly.
Louise's Shutting Service #581	Before I take the kids to school (if it is my day) I walk around the house turning off light switches even if someone is in the room (a pre-emptive measure, since I know they won't shut it off when they leave). I do this sweep before dinner, too, and other random times. I also close the kitchen cabinets and drawers, which, after any meal or coffee refill, Nick leaves wide open, like someone ransacked our kitchen. If I'm annoyed (a pretty good chance) I will slam and sigh.
Read-On-Demand, #5,174	Either Nick or I must read one of the four *Wings of Fire* series comic books out loud to Bruce at least five times a day, for a minimum of twenty minutes. The synopsis is five dragons who must save the world, and it's pretty compelling; however, reading comics out loud is hard because one constantly has to tell Bruce who in the comic is speaking, and has to explain words such as "Rrrroooaaarrrrr" and "Accckggurglgurgl"

Dillons #0090	-$21.89 Emotional-support 24-pack of La Croix, frozen-chocolate-covered-raspberries that are outrageously costly, like eating fruit covered in melted gold. Nick used to hound me about spending frivolously like this, but I think he's given up.
Overpriced Outdoor-ish Clothing Company	-$51 plus shipping I buy myself a Christmas present from Nick, since I know exactly what I want: another fleece vest (this one is blue, zip-up, with a hood) to go with my collection of vests. They compliment yoga pants perfectly, and reduce my feeling of over-exposure in just a thin T-shirt, where my stomach is too visible, I think.
Nick's Photo Service, Market Edition #43	When the grocery store doesn't have, say, pepitas, frozen cubed butternut squash, or whatever item is on the list I hand him, Nick has started taking picture of the empty shelf. "This proves I did look for it so you can't say I didn't," he says.

ETSY.com	-$22.40
	A forest green infinity scarf for my sister-in-law for Christmas. I decide to keep it for myself --- I need something to wear for the annual family photo, which is tonight. After finding Bruce's one "dress" shirt (i.e. with a collar and buttons) and helping Olive assemble her outfit of a denim jacket and tulle skirt, we all drive to the spot Nick has picked out, Bruce complaining of hunger pangs the whole time. The spot is a field on Nick's running route, and after trudging out there, he says, "It looks better in the morning light. That's when I see it. Let's try a different spot." I complain about walking in my grey suede booties, which I never wear because they make my ankles fold. After walking to the new spot (just another field, by the way), Nick declares this is too much of a pain (something about how he hates posing us all and then setting the timer, running to his place, etc. etc.) and we should just go home. "I'll find a new spot and we'll do it another day," he says.

"Nope. We do it now or never," I say. We grimly pose.

I haven't seen how the photo turned out yet, but I did decide to give the scarf to my sister-in-law after all. It doesn't look that great on me. |
| Hotel Krug, Stay # 200 | I let Nick sleep in on a Saturday while I take the kids to get their flu shots. I have to lean on Olive's arms with all my weight so the nurse can get to her thigh. We go to Paradise Donuts afterwards and get Nick two donuts, one that he eats and one of which I eat at 10 p.m. after thinking about it all day. |

DAYLIGHT DONUTS, Topeka KS	-$33.96 A friend mentions she brought donuts to the faculty at her kid's school, and that sounded like something I want to do. I call the night before, place my order, and then we all swing by the shop before school in the morning. I have the warm boxes on my lap and go to open the top one, wanting to enjoy the delicious satisfaction of a good deed, but Nick places his hand on top. "Are you crazy? People don't want you breathing all over their donuts, Louise. Get a grip!" I stew.
Westlake Hardware, Topeka KS #089	-$21.82 Lawn bags. Nick and I rake leaves. It's satisfying, watching our stuffed lawn bags stack up in the alley. If you would have told me I'd willingly do yard work as an adult, I would have laughed uncontrollably.
PETCO, Topeka KS	-$15.19 Crickets for Stripes, our gecko that lives in an aquarium in Bruce's room. Stripes was a Covid purchase that was my idea last March. Unfortunately, I didn't think about what geckos eat (live crickets) until after we bought Stripes. Nick feeds Stripes (because I certainly won't), which means buying a supply of crickets every week (they smell, by the way) and using a pair of giant tweezers to dangle them into his cage. Nick also scoops his poop from the sand and replaces his water.

HAPPY HOUR, Lawrence, KS	-$21.59 When Nick has a photo assignment in Lawrence, he gets his beer there.
THE MERC, Lawrence KS	-$6.55 I benefit from a Lawrence trip by him bringing back a spinach, walnut, and goat cheese salad from the fancy co-op. Sometimes I have to ask him to bring this back, this time I did not.
Dillons #9007 Topeka KS	-$65.66 Included, but not limited to: A tub of vegetable shortening for my new tortilla-making habit, which Nick supports. He probably likes my baking because it's cheap and produces results. Also, I get two more sacks of brown rice, which he dislikes but will eat.

Scheduling of Sex #1,065	It's one thing to talk about *when* we want to have sex --- Nick and I use the euphemism "hang out" so we can discuss it in front of the kids (say, when we're cleaning the kitchen after dinner and the kids eat their allotted three pieces of leftover Halloween candy, whose pile is growing alarmingly smaller by the day because of us). One of us just says, "Hey, want to hang out tomorrow before lunch?" And the other person says, "Sure!" But how to do it without spoiling the mood, especially now when we both work from home and share an office? Example: Me, across the room: "Do you have a sec?" Nick: "Sure, let me just send this email and get some more coffee." Me (starts getting undressed): "O.K., see you in five, and I have a Zoom at noon, so…"
Tacos El Sol, Topeka KS	Nick and I get tacos from a restaurant in East Topeka once a week. Lately, the tacos at this place have been tasting a little like dish soap.
PETSMART, Topeka KS	-$15.81 More crickets
Backpedaling about Stripes #27	After the kids are in bed, I remind Nick again that the pet store told us if things didn't work out with Stripes, we were welcome to bring him back there, no questions asked. I have reminded him of this many times since we brought him home and he hid under his heat rock, where he stays, always. Crickets crawl in, they don't crawl out. Finally, Nick caves, and the next day he packs up Stripes in a plastic carrier and heads to his car. The kids are jumping on the trampoline in the backyard and see him pass, but

	don't say a word. It takes another three days for them to ask about Stripes.

Now

"What are you really doing when you look him up?" your therapist asks. She is talking about an ex-boyfriend, the French one, the relationship that disintegrated during the time I had brain surgery.

"I'm looking for clues about who he is now, about why it's good we didn't stay together, looking at his wife, which makes me feel terrible about myself, because she is tiny and beautiful."

My therapist interrupts, "But you know nothing about her, what kind of trauma she may have been through. Pictures mean very little."

That doesn't convince me, though. The wife looks pretty happy to me. She looks happy and symmetrical.

How to Talk About God With a Personal Trainer

My personal trainer's name was Ed. Actually, it was Mohammed, but it was understandable that he chose to go by Ed because of, well, Kansas. America, too. He was from Dubai, which he said was like another planet. I believed him.

He had a pretty thick accent, and said things like "more two" instead of "two more." Totally hunky, with short, curly black hair and big arm muscles. What they call soulful eyes. Probably my age. He had me doing all kinds of exercises: throwing a medicine ball on a trampoline, lifting heavy ropes, running and touching cones, and, of course, sit-ups—on an exercise ball, on the floor, on a downward-facing bench. Endless sit ups. When I said I hated working my abs the most of any body part he looked at me and said, "I can tell."

I was very embarrassed that I had a personal trainer at all, and told no one except Nick. Whenever I was telling a story to a friend and it would involve working out, which seemed to happen quite often, I would have to edit myself and switch "personal trainer" to "friend," such as, "When I was talking to my....friend at the gym."

*

"What is Dubai like?" I said to Ed.
"It's hot," he said.
"But it's hot here," I said. (It was August in Kansas).
"No, it's not," he said.

*

He said in his culture, mothers were second after God, which I heard as "second after dogs."

*

He shook his head a lot at me.
"What did you have for lunch yesterday?" he would ask.
"A turkey sandwich," I said.
"Not bad," he said. "Was there cheese on that sandwich?"
"Um, yes?" I said.
"And mayo?"
"Yes."
"Hmmm," he would say.

*

I always asked him what he ate. He said he had cottage cheese and oatmeal for breakfast, and steak and a sweet potato for lunch and dinner. He and his wife ate plain yogurt before bed.

*

"What's that on your shirt?" he said.
"Oh, it's chocolate. I wore this shirt last night too." I said.

*

He asked me once if I could get him in a program at my university that would certify him to be an English as a Second Language instructor. I asked around, and we didn't have a program like that. I remember how sad he looked when I told him. Almost like he didn't believe me, too.

He wasn't my first trainer. My first was a young woman named Laura who was a vegan who had lost 75 pounds. I liked her and would have still been with her if we hadn't moved to a nearby town, but we did. At my new gym, I was assigned to Ed.

I thought a personal trainer was a good idea, though. The woman next to me at yoga had asked if I was pregnant last month. I wasn't, and couldn't fit into any of my old clothes I'd worn before I'd had Bruce, which was more than a year ago. I learned a lot about Ed, because when someone is watching me work out, it turns out I like to ask questions. I found out that he had two big dogs, two children in middle school (I remember them being step-children, but I could be wrong) that he thought were lazy. He didn't let his dogs inside the house, though. Maybe that's a cultural thing? But I was always a little bit uncomfortable with Ed. Or maybe it's more accurate to say I always felt like he wanted me to be a little more fit than I had any intention of being. Like, when Ed said that I might want to wear looser pants. Or he could see that I'd been eating M &Ms again.

He made me do these balancing exercises that I hated. I had to close my eyes and first try to balance on one foot, then reach out and touch my nose, then try to do a tree pose from yoga. Then I had to do it balancing on the other foot. I was always so embarrassed to be seen doing this, and I was always embarrassed anyway because I was working out with a trainer, while the other gym goers were smart enough to go it alone. But Ed insisted that the balance exercises were necessary because I had had brain surgery, and we needed to re-train my body. He was probably right. But I still hated them.

*

Half the time I would cancel my session, texting him from my bed at 6 a.m. " Stayed up too late last night grading!" or "Bruce was up a lot last night!", both of which were sometimes true. Sometimes I just didn't want to go. He was always understanding.

*

Once, I said I wasn't sure if I believed in God. He never really took me seriously after that, and he couldn't let it go, bringing it up each time we met. I tried to make it better by saying things like, "I didn't say I definitely don't, I'm just not sure," and saying, "I just have a lot of questions, but he didn't buy it. "I guess you don't care where you go after you die," he said.

*

So I called it quits. It was expensive. And early in the morning. But I kept hearing Ed's voice in my head every time I added cream to my coffee or cheese to a sandwich. More accurately, I saw him shaking his head and smiling. Quitting was difficult, maybe because I felt I had to explain my reasons to him, and he would hold up both hands in response and say, "It's O.K., it's O.K." Once, a few months after I left, I got a text from him, saying he hoped I was doing well. I responded that I was, and it was true.

*

Sometimes I think up imaginary texts to send him: "Jazzercise has helped my balance!"
"I finally started drinking my coffee black!"
"I subbed mustard for mayo!"
Or I would have questions for him,
"Do you still have those giant dogs you used to talk about?"
"How are your wife and kids (stepkids? I'll never know)?
and, "How can you be so sure about the God thing?"

Now

"How did you feel you when your parents got divorced?" my therapist asks.

"Relieved," I say. "It didn't really affect me like it did my brothers, who were younger."

"Sometimes, some of the trauma from divorce happens with children before the break-up takes place. What was life at your house like then?" she says.

My main complaint—only one, really—about my therapist's office space itself is the lack of windows. There are none. The office is on the inside of a hallways in a large three-story building. But the walls are painted an apple green, and she has strategically placed fidgets on the side table beside the chair where I sit. Also, a full box of tissues. It is cozy in here.

"My mom was gone a lot in the year or two before the divorce," I say, and my dad was working, twisting a metal fidget, shaped like an insect. "She hired a Mrs. Doubtfire-like babysitter, whose name was Mrs. Knapp. Mrs. Knapp wore her hair in pink plastic rollers until lunchtime, and brought her own English Breakfast teabags—which she used twice each—with her. Also her transistor radio. Her favorite song was "Pennies From Heaven."

I could have kept going. I could have talked about Mrs. Knapp's husband, Mr. Jim, who was silent but drove her to our house sometimes or else sat at home in his recliner. I could have talked about her love of Live with Regis and Kathie Lee, which we watched religiously every morning. I could have talked about how she always made us two things to eat: Banana hors d'oeuvres (slices of bananas with dollops of peanut butter) or tomato soup served in a mug. Three things: if it was dinner, then Lemon Chicken. Her daughter Missy who lived in Atlanta. Her blue flowered housecoat. How she gently said, to my mom every time she was about to leave, "Put a little lipstick on."

"But where did she go, your mother? When Mrs. Knapp stayed with you?" my therapist says.

"She was on the town's tennis team. When I think of that now, that seems so foreign (Topeka doesn't have a tennis team that I know of, other than at the Country Club, and if it did, of course I would never be on it, as I don't play tennis, or any sport)."

She made new friends who were also on the tennis team. Cindy, who drove a red convertible and had nails to match. Karen, who had a daughter about my age at the time. The daughter and I didn't "vibe," and I remember once we went to the mall with our moms and Cheryl got her makeup and her daughter cried, not recognizing her.

How to Dance

When I started going to Jazzercise, I planned on hanging around after class to tell the instructor about my balance. But I didn't. I forgot, or she would be talking to another woman, dabbing the sweat from her own forehead with a towel, and I left it for next class. I kept leaving it, like it was a chore that can be undone forever. Like cleaning grout with a toothbrush. Something that should be done but never is.

I was the youngest person in the 10:30 a.m. Jazzercise class, but I liked it that way. I was 38. Mostly everyone else in the 10:30 class also wanted to march in place instead of jog, and shuffle instead of skip. I couldn't really run or skip because one leg was weaker than the other. Some of the steps eluded us because of sheer complicatedness, like the Heel Hop, or the Back Shuffle. A lot of us struggled, half doing the moves, trying to stay in step. But we kept going.

When Jazzercise came up in conversation, almost everyone I talked to thought I was joking, and said they thought it vanished long ago, like Sweatin' to the Oldies with Richard Simmons. But no. It never went away. Jazzercise was like the Jane Fonda tapes I did with my mom when I was a kid. There were similar steps: the Grapevine, Chassé, lunges. I had balance issues because of brain surgeries I had in my early twenties, so keeping my body strong was something I thought about. But I got bored exercising, so every year or so I tried something new. For the last six months before Jazz (as I came to call it) I was walking the trails at the state park, but after a few months I kept checking my watch more and more and the minutes seemed longer and longer, and I knew it was time for a change.

There was a summer when I was ten or eleven when I did Jane Fonda tapes a lot. Or I guess it wasn't Jane Fonda, because that would have been years earlier, when I did it with my mom, back when our only T.V. was in the basement and my two younger brothers would be playing with toys all around us lying on the floor and scissoring our legs. This, when I was a pre-teen, was Cindy Crawford's *Shape Your Body*. When I was six, I got *Get In Shape, Girl*, a "toy" exercise kit—an exercise audio tape (I forgot there was such a thing!), a sweatband, blue, with a pink cursive slogan, "Get in shape, girl!" and wristbands. I mostly just wore the sweatband as a headband—there is a picture of me wearing it in a pile of Michigan fall leaves. But the video *Shape Your Body* is what I remember most. Cindy in that white one-piece, standing on the beach, and me in my black Umbro shorts and Garfield T-shirt, standing on the family-room carpet (we had a T.V. upstairs by that time, with a glass of orange juice and ice (the choices in our house were tap water, orange juice, and milk), the high-bass music pumping as we did our crunches. By we I mean Cindy and me. Most of the time I wouldn't make it through the whole workout and felt guilty when I switched it off, but that soon passed. There were so many more workout videos to come, all of which I did a few times: Gabrielle Reece, Billy Blanks, Denise Austin, Jillian Michaels. Later there was a prenatal yoga one that I did ten minutes of and switched off, never to do again. While workout tapes are magnetic, it is rare for me (or probably most people) to actually do one the whole way through. It's just so easy to quit.

My favorite spot in the 10:30 class was on one side of the room or the other, so I could reach out and touch the wall for balance help. I liked to be about halfway back—I would never be caught dead in the front row (way too risky), but I heard that if you danced in the very back row you burned fewer calories than if you were in a middle row because you put in less effort. Plus, folks in the last couple of rows are usually gone by the end of the hour-long class—those ladies left early before the stretching cool-down began. They tended to talk, cackle, even, and they brought coffee in to-go cups instead of water. There was one woman who checked her phone—in her purse hanging on a hook—nearly every song.

It's usually women who came to the class, but not always. There was one man, stooped over with a full head of white hair, named Bob, and he came quite often. There was also a young man with a ponytail who showed up every now and then. When I mentioned either of these men to Nick, usually at dinner, he laughed and said, "Why do you always mention it if a guy is in class?" and, really, I didn't know. Maybe I liked seeing people who were a bit out of place, like I was?

I brought my kids sometimes, who were 8 and 4 at the time. There was a playroom, but they could stand outside the doorway and watch, too. On the drive home one day I asked them how my dancing was, and Olive said, "You almost looked like everyone else, Mom."

The "almost" bothered me for a second, and I was disappointed. I wanted to be indistinguishable. But I knew what she said was true, generous, even. I decided to take it as a compliment, because I knew my daughter meant it as one. It's true, also, that not everyone in Jazzercise knows all the steps and can do all the moves perfectly. Not at all. But for some reason I wanted to be that way. And my daughter knew that somehow.

The instructors were interesting, too. One of my favorites was Elaine, who had a tattoo sleeve on one arm and glasses. She was petite and cheerful, and had six kids, the youngest was a baby that someone watched in the nursery. Tamara, who clapped a lot and modified one routine to the country song "She Thinks My Tractor's Sexy." There was Emily, who had been a friend of mine before I started attending class. She made up lyrics to the songs, and once had to pee so bad that she had to leave in the middle of the routine. Luckily she remembered to turn off her mic. I did say something to Emily once, after the first couple of weeks, about my balance, and she said I could always make a modification to make the moves easier, and I said that wouldn't be necessary. Why did I say that?

Most often heard word? "Squeeze!" Second was "booty."

In the 10:30 a.m. class, when most people were at work, I got to know the regulars. There was a short woman with a bowl cut and large purple glasses, Also, a woman who was always in the front row. She wore her mid-length hair down and was always brightly lipsticked in shades of magenta. She stood, even when the rest of us were doing abs on our backs, wriggling on the floor. She just stepped side-to-side until we were done. Some of the older women didn't like to get down on the ground, but once you decided that, Emily said, "it's over."

I tried to time my entrance so I came in right when class began. If I came in too early, I had to stand around and check my phone. A lot of the women knew each other and stood around in groups of three or four. Once, I asked Emily how some of the women got to be so good. She said, "Well, some of them have been coming for ten years." On New Year's Day there was a special class, and the people with the highest attendance got a prize. One woman had come to class every day, sometimes twice a day, for the entire year. Like 403 days. She got a rubber bracelet. I got a T-shirt along with a bunch of other folks, for coming a certain number of times. I think it was then, once I got that tank top, which said "Goal Getter" and which I started wear often, that I decided not to tell anyone else about my balance. Maybe I was good enough.

When it got too hard, I thought about leaving class before it was over, and the only reason I didn't was if I did it once, I was afraid I would leave early every time. Sometimes, I got frustrated. The balance work, where we did ballet-like moves like *arabesque* and *tondue*, especially killed me. As the months wore on, I realized that if I rested a minute, no one cared. As that was a revelation.

Sometimes I didn't feel like bouncing my hip in a sassy way, or doing a pelvic circle. But I did it anyway. I didn't know how long I would keep coming. I'd never done a workout for ten years straight, that's for sure. But it was the closest I'd come to dancing since my brain surgeries. And that was something.

Now

Times passes. Nick, the kids, and I go on a long trip, having to do with my presenting something at a conference in Spain. After a day at the beach, at the Air B & B, sunburned and peaceful, I block the ex's Facebook and immediately feel better. The next day, I text my therapist and tell her I'm going in a different direction and sign off as "Warmly."

I see an advertisement for a plastic surgeon in Houston who works with people with facial paralysis. His technique takes nerves from another spot on the body, like the ankle, and somehow transplants them to the paralyzed area, splicing them with one of the cranial nerves. Cool, I think. Then I get sad. It never ends, this want.

How to Find a Chiro

I needed to see a chiropractor—I was scared but desperate. Visions of necks snapping like chicken bones kept popping up; I remembered the only chiropractor I had ever known, a college roommate. He had been an opera major. That hadn't worked out for him, and he had joined his dad's chiropractic practice after graduating. He had been a terrible roommate—always bringing friends home from the bars after last call, and they would have sing-alongs while he played the guitar on the deck right outside my bedroom window. His friends were mostly other opera majors, and their shrieking was louder than the usual drunken shrieking.

Anyway.

I Googled a chiropractor whom a friend said was "magic." I trusted this friend because she, too, had a healthy distrust of chiropractors, being married to an ex-Mormon whose parents took him to a chiropractor for everything.

"And I mean everything. If he had a fever? Chiropractor. Earache? Chiropractor. It's a wonder I ever went to one at all," my friend said. She had gone for a sore right wrist that she couldn't shake. Apparently, the magic chiropractor had slathered her wrist in Bio-Freeze, and hooked it up to an E-stim machine (something that had electrodes that delivered tiny shocks to muscles, and that was good somehow). He also used some other electronic doodad that he controlled from his phone.

Now her wrist was good as new, she said, waggling her fingers.

"He's a person-who-hates-chiropractors chiropractor."

His name was Dr. Sprock, but I kept saying it "Spock" in my head. Instead of calling to make an appointment, it was done by text. Sessions were in fifteen-minute slots. My kind of doctor.

*

I had back spasms. The last one had been triggered by pulling clothes out of the washing machine. When I had felt my back tighten up and then turn into a white-hot knot, I couldn't help but cry out, which scared Bruce, my son, 6. He had started crying, and then we were both crying. I had hobbled to the bed and held Bruce's hand until Nick got home from a run. Useless for days, I was. Months later, when I twisted my ankle and was lying next to Bruce on the floor, waiting for my neighbor to come help me up, he said, "At least you didn't yell this time."

*

The day of my first appointment with Dr Sprock, I pulled into the parking lot that Siri had led me to, but saw no sign indicating this was the place. An electric blue Mustang was the only car there.

After poking around a couple of empty hallways, I went in another door and saw a tan, handsome, bro-ish looking man in khakis and a tight polo shirt. "You found it!" he said. "I keep meaning to put a sign up, but I just moved in like yesterday."

There was no receptionist, nothing else in the empty room besides a couple of chairs. Behind him was another room with what looked like a massage chair. He motioned for me to come in.

I explained that I'd never been to a chiropractor before, and was kind of nervous, and he nodded and motioned for me to remove my glasses.

"Earrings too, and your watch, take it all off," he said.

I remembered thinking, oh, so we're already to that step.

*

Days later, when I was telling my mom about the chiropractor, my mom tried to convince me that pelvic floor exercises were the answer. We were on vacation at our family cabin in Colorado, a 100-year-old firetrap that wasn't winterized and had a severe mouse problem. Over coffee before anyone else was up, in a kitchen so cold we huddled around an open oven, turned on, Mom went on and on about different routines I could do and how it would change my life ("You can do these sitting at your desk and no one will ever know!" Mom said, pouring another cup). The only way I could think to change the subject was to show Mom the bottle of alfalfa supplements I had bought from Dr. Sprock—and to tell her they had kelp in them, too. Mom shrugged and said, "You never know what will help."

Mom was the only person I knew who drank Kombucha purely for the taste. She still did yoga to a DVD and slept with her windows open in the middle of winter. She was very DIY when it came to health. Her husband, a doctor, ran 10 miles easily but regularly ate Sonic and Girl Scout Cookies, so who did know, indeed.

*

The only time during that first appointment when I felt hesitant was when the chiropractor gathered me up in his arms like a baby. It was for an adjustment, but I felt a little uncomfortable. Not that something would happen, exactly, but that I had never been that close to someone so brawny. So much bigger than I was, maybe. Nick was very strong—he hauled recliners up flights of stairs, rebuilt porches, and climbed ladders while carrying tools, but I was pretty sure I weighed about the same as him. Maybe more, if I was being super honest. When I was putting my glasses and earrings back on, the chiropractor and I made small talk. He said he and his buddies were going on a trip to Branson that weekend, which they did every year, and they were excited to sing karaoke, but he never did.

"I always sit and watch," he said.

I thought that was sad, and wondered if he had someone, but figured if he did, that someone would be going to Branson with him. I had decided that the electric blue Mustang in the parking lot was his. I handed him my credit card and he put it in a contraption attached to his phone. I was happy with myself—I had done it! Gone to the appointment and he hadn't broken my neck! I felt lighter, and giddy, the way I felt after completing a task I dreaded. I made another appointment with him for next week right then, and bought those alfalfa supplements. He told me to take them right before bed, "so they'll soak in while you sleep." I nodded, like that made sense. The pills had no coating, and the directions said to take three at a time, so I choked them down.

*

As I was turning to leave after my adjustments were over that next week, he told me he was excited because the pizza place he liked had a two-for-the-price-of-one special, and he was going to get it and eat pizza on his couch that night. All by himself.

"You eat pizza?" I said.

"Sure," he said.

"That's hilarious," I said, and laughed. But really I felt sad for him again. In my imagination, doctors, even chiropractors, always had partners and social lives and ate plated, rainbow-colored food at a leisurely dinner each evening, followed by a dessert of sorbet. But I also knew this wasn't true. My ophthalmologist was single and slept on his couch. He had told me so at my last appointment—an aside to some story about wine tasting, one of his hobbies.

*

The next time I went to Dr. Sprock, it had been a while. Months. It was fall, and I had started water aerobics (life changing, said another friend with back problems. It was fun, but it also made me feel very old), but then I felt a twinge in my back while getting up one morning, and after debating it with myself out loud for 30 minutes while making breakfast and getting Nick and the kids out the door, I decided to go. I got on my phone, made the appointment, drove across town, and walked in to Dr. Sprock's office with a big smile.

"Hi!" I said, breezing into his exam room, slipping off my earrings, laying down on the table getting comfortable.

"How have you been? Pizza lately? Ha!"

"I'm sorry," he said, teeth so bright they looked a little blue. "Name? What's the issue?"

I was crushed, but got businesslike quickly. Sometimes I did that with people. Got over familiar, assumed I meant something to someone when I didn't. No biggie. It happens, and remember, I said to myself—doctors see lots of patients. They can't be expected to remember everyone they treat.

Lying face-down on the table, Dr. Sprock rubbed some cooling ointment on me and started the E-stim machine. While it pulsed, I thought about, as a teacher, there were lots of times where I would recognize a former student's face but not know their name at all, or maybe remember it hours later. Other times it was the opposite, and a student would know me but I wouldn't know them back. One of my former students had been my server at a BBQ restaurant, and it wasn't until halfway thorough the meal that he shyly reminded me. Former students were everywhere, at Target, the public library, the grocery store, and I never felt bad about not remembering them, just happy that there were people in the world that touched my arm and said "Remember me?" as that was one of my favorite things. To greet someone out of the blue. To know someone, however hazily.

"Plus, we all know they're not really doctors anyway," I thought. "Chiropractor school is more like a certification program." But that didn't make me feel any better. I didn't know why.

Now

"What do you think?" I ask Nick, after I see that he read the link for the new-smile plastic surgeon's website I sent him from across the room. The kids are watching their nighttime TV show right before bed, zombies with wet hair and ice cream mustaches. We had been through this before—surgeries with less-than-desirable results. The last one was fifteen years ago.

"I think you're perfect," he says. "But if you want to contact him, you can. But I don't want you to get hurt. Disappointed."

I sit next to him. "Yeah," I say. "That would suck."

I email the surgeon that night.

How to Make a Praise Sandwich

From the Conflict Resolution for Couples Webinar: Use the "Praise Sandwich" template when you feel close to criticizing your partner. Also, try to use an "I" statement when conflict arises (Example: "I feel like your sister when you don't close the bathroom door to take care of business.")

Me talking to Nick:

1.   Lead with a compliment: "I'm glad you are able to sleep so deeply."

2.   Share concern: "Me waking you up every morning makes me feel like I am your mother, as I wake up our children for school at the same time."

3.   Provide encouragement and support: "I bet you can set an alarm clock! I can show you how, but I bet you already know how, as you look at your phone quite a lot these days. Can I get you a bigger alarm? Louder?"

1.   Lead with a compliment: "It's so cool that you are very methodical about where you put your personal items."

2.   Share concern: "It's hard to have Taco Night when your keys, wallet, glasses, and pocket detritus like pennies and receipts are on the kitchen counter."

3.   Provide encouragement and support: "Maybe you can find another place to empty your pockets? I can show you a good spot! Here it is, your very own dresser, which is conveniently in our bedroom, where you can put all your belongings because it is a room dedicated to you! (Or carry a man-bag and hang it on a hook? Or leave most of your shit in your car?)"

1.   Lead with a compliment: "It's great that you don't place too much emphasis on material items."

2.   Share concern: "But I feel frustrated when you are now asking me what we should get your mom for Christmas, as it is only a few days away. I have already had several phone conversations with her, weeks ago, about what she wants, which I then told you about then went and bought (a new frying pan for her morning egg, two new cookie sheets, (which, by the way, are strangely very heavy—remember when I asked you to guess how much they weighed, to see if she would be able to lift them with one arm? And you laughed at me and said she's not an invalid?); I also made her a framed photo of her and the

kids in Santa hats from last Christmas; Lastly, flannel pajamas, red and white striped)."

3. Provide encouragement and support: "I know how you can help! Here is some wrapping paper and tape! I will show you to the basement, where there is a lot of space to wrap gifts."

1. Lead with a compliment: Sigh…

Now

I mentally rearrange my summer schedule so I can fly out to Houston and have the surgery. I call my dentist and make plans to have my teeth whitened. I feel like I haven't smiled with teeth for a long, long time outside my little circle of friends and my students, who make me laugh daily.

How to Quit

Things my classmates talked about in spin class:

1. How to make bourbon slush
2. What causes strokes
3. Someone's dad who had a stroke
4. Steak tartare
5. Roofs caving in

    We rode our bikes in a circle, which wasn't how spin classes usually sat, I had found. It was probably so everyone could talk to each other, which was new to me, too. Everyone gabbed non-stop. In other classes, everyone had their head down, and the music throbbed, lights low. In here, at the Y, music was from Pandora on the teacher's phone, and it was always different, sometimes The Beach Boys, sometimes Otis Redding or Justin Beiber, but it was never what you would describe as loud.

    I started the spin class because I had quit my weight-lifting class. Before that had been a short stint at the gym by my house, before that a 10 months with a personal trainer, before that I had been pregnant and swimming laps, and if I wanted to count backward, I could name a lot more fitness trends I had tried. My mom was a master exerciser. My parents had a Nordic Track and a rowing machine. When their marriage was almost over, my mom would go for long walks after a fight. She was also on a tennis team, and played on that for years, owning a closetful of white pleated skirts and bright polos.

*

    My weight-lifting class met in this old brick warehouse on the east part of town called Oakland. It was by Little Russia, which had an infamous deli that served turkey sandwiches with hot pickles and had employees who yelled at you. This was where the trees of the tree-lined streets were giant and the houses small and tired. I had found this class by searching "weight lifting" and my city online, and had seen an article in the local paper featuring Gil, the teacher, who had been selling t-shirts with weight-lifting slogans to raise money for a client with cancer. The slogans had made me uncomfortable, ones like, "Eat Big, Lift Heavy, Fuck Hard."

*

    Food was a main subject where my mom and I differed. Nick and I had learned to bring backup boxes of macaroni and cheese for the kids if we were visiting my mom and stepdad, as my mom usually made something like gazpacho or watermelon salad. On a family vacation, we were making spaghetti for six and my mom boiled half a box of noodles.

"The box said there were eight servings in here, and two of us are children!" she had said when I complained. Her lunch now was diced pears over Greek yogurt, no honey. "It's just what I like," she said, and shrugged.

*

When I first drove to the weight-lifting warehouse it had been windy, and when I went over the second bridge, I feared my car might blow away. At the brick shell of a building, before I opened the door I heard clinking weights and grunts. Inside, I saw a couple of high-school aged kids in sweatsuits spot each other on a bench and a big, bearded man whom I recognized from the newspaper article photo as Gil. After I introduced myself, I explained what I was looking for: balance, getting back to "normal."

"I'll make a plan and we'll get started," Gil said. "Nothing's better for the body."

I drove to the store for weight gloves later that day.

*

Once, my mom said to me, "You know, it's O.K. to be hungry."

A quote of hers that Nick and I later repeated to make each other laugh: "You've always had a healthy amount of body odor."

*

When I went on walks, I didn't go through my own neighborhood with the red brick streets and pretty historic houses. I quickly turned out to a sidewalk and went towards an equally old, but more forgotten, part of town. I had to keep looking down to make sure not to trip on the uneven sidewalk. Lots of these houses had little dogs who yapped in small fenced front yards, and empty cigarette packs or soda cans in the border between the sidewalk and the street. Then the sidewalk ran out and I could see the highway, past a yellow field. I liked walking out there where no one was, wearing God knows what: ancient winter hats, sunglasses, too-short yoga pants. Who cared? Who was there to see?

*

I started going to the weight-lifting class three mornings a week at 5:30 with a mixture of happiness and dread. Happiness because it was nice to do the lifts: the squat, the bench press, deadlift, bent-over-row, and push press. I was feeling good because I was getting exercise but not wasting my life on the elliptical machine, watching old home-remodeling shows on my phone. When I arrived, I had to give Gil a notebook and he would write my workout down. In addition to the weight-lifting moves I knew, there were new things: the rowing machine, kettleball swings, and the Simply Horrible. For this, I had to run down a gravel road dragging a tire that was tied around my waist. It was the kind of thing where old men in pickup trucks would slow down and yell,

"Tired?" out the window.

But after a few weeks, then months, there was something about having to give the notebook to Gil each morning that I didn't like, that I would in fact fear, something about how he would be talking to another lifter and I would have to stand there and wait until he was finished to silently hand the notebook to him. It seemed like I would stand there for hours. Gil seemed to always have plenty to chat about with the other people there, but never me. Sometimes he would gruffly ask, "How's school?" because he knew I was a professor but that was it. On my end, I could never think of anything more to say than, "Great!"

My body didn't seem to be changing, and my balance was the same as it always was: poor. I still slammed shoulders into doorways sometimes or wavered when getting up from the kitchen table. But I couldn't bring it up to Gil. I couldn't imagine bringing anything up to him, at this point.

*

Or maybe it was how Gil would sometimes be late, and when he arrived I would pretend to be busy, doing push-ups, but really I had been looking at my phone.

*

Now, my mom was into playing Pickleball, a team had formed in her small town, and they met on a neighborhood park's tennis courts. She also had a room in her house with some yoga stuff and a Peloton. A personal trainer came on the screen and told you what to do.

*

The other people in the warehouse were more experienced than I, and they all followed a different workout written on a large marker board. A few guys spotted each other through their sets, and they liked heavy metal music and they liked it loud. This was where I ran into trouble, because I often had to talk to Gil to get instructions on how to do a certain exercise he had written down in my notebook, like Farmer's Walk, or clarification on his handwriting (was that "Russian Twists" or "Scissor Kicks")? Gil was usually walking around with an old broom handle he used sort of a cane, only not for support but for fun. He still competed as a powerlifter. I would ask him my question and he would shout his answer over the music, and usually I would have to ask "what?" and so he would shout it again, and sometimes I understood, but sometimes I didn't and just nodded, turned around, and started doing whatever I thought he'd said.

*

Weight-lifting class was not fun anymore, and I told Nick as much. Part of it was the heavy metal songs.

"Why don't you just ask them to turn the music down?" he said. I made a face.

Part of the warehouse floor was dedicated to the CrossFitters, who had a separate teacher who paid Gil to let him use the space. The small group of four or five people were unfailingly in motion: jumping on top of wooden boxes, doing burpees, or rolling giant tires down the gravel road. They were always drenched in sweat and stopped only to bend over, put their hands on their knees, and look like they were going to puke.

*

One day I just never went back to weight lifting. My notebook and gloves are probably still there in the cubby. I felt freed, and that was how I ended up at the spin class at the Y, riding spin bikes in a circle arrangement, talking about whatever struck our fancy. I quit after a few weeks, though.

Months later, when Nick and I were taking a walk on the grounds of a former mental hospital that was now closed, we talked about my weightlifting class, and I said, "Why do you think it was so awkward? Why did it go south after a while? I really can't remember."

The grass was long, bleached, and shimmering, and the trees, unpruned for years since this place had closed in the 1990s, had scraggly limbs that reached toward the sky.

"I think in the beginning, that guy thought that he could help you, and he was excited, but after a while he realized that it wasn't going to fix your balance or other issues, and so he just ignored you," Nick said.

"That's sad. I don't like thinking about that," I said.

"I don't want to make you sad. But those guys, they're all about cheering each other on and making gains, but sometimes that's not possible," Nick said. "Sometimes, no one can help."

I agreed. And I felt a little lost. I had not gone to spin class at the Y for long either, and I didn't miss it. I didn't miss the people. I hadn't stayed for long enough to learn anybody's name, even though they seemed like interesting folks. I don't know why I quit so many things. I didn't miss the dark, early morning drives to the weight-lifting class, either—it had been in a part of town where there weren't street lights, and my headlights sometimes lit up a figure walking on the sidewalk, probably going to catch a bus, but then they were gone in a second, and my car would be back alone, back in the darkness again.

How to Be a Passenger

One winter, years earlier, I rode to a different weight lifting class with Lisa, who worked in the business office. I had stopped driving after a car accident that spring, and needed a way to get to weight-lifting class. Weight lifting would be good for my balance issues, a yoga teacher had told me. I had trouble with my balance since my brain surgeries and was always looking for something that might help.

I would change from teaching clothes into workout wear in the bathroom, which always stank and had water on the floor. Then I would trudge, head down against the wind, across campus to Lisa's building. Lisa's office was hot, and she had large legs and an old car. Lisa told stories about when she was a young married mother living in Paris. She would take her little baby on cheap flights to Scotland or Italy, just because. Her baby girl grew up and went to Brown but didn't like it, so now she was living at home.

During the weight-lifting class picnic that summer, I said how delicious the food was, and Lisa said, "Well, you're sure eating enough of it to know."

I had stopped getting rides from Lisa at that point, anyway. By then, I rode to class with a woman named Chris. Chris worked part time at a power plant. She and her husband lived in a funky log cabin with metal yard decorations and colored garden balls everywhere. Chris dyed her hair red and wore overalls. Getting pregnant and married at 17 was the best thing that ever happened to her, she said. She asked me how much my husband, Nick, and I paid for our house, and I told her.

Sometimes I would have days where I could drive. Never far, but the two minutes it took to get downtown or to the Kroger. It was so freeing, it was like I had taken a drug, like I was just living in the now, that nothing else mattered, and I was happier than I'd ever been. But that feeling would evaporate. All it took was one second of my foot not finding the brake pedal, or hearing a horn, and then I couldn't sit in the driver's seat without shaking. Then it would be back to square one.

After Chris, for years I rode to weight lifting with Eileen. Often, Eileen needed to go by the grocery store after class. Sometimes we would go to the co-op that had kale salads to-go, organic beauty products, and wooden earrings. Eileen would insist on buying me a coconut-milk ice-cream sandwich, Eileen's favorite treat, and I would happily protest and then give in.

When I would talk to my mom on the phone and mention I wasn't driving, she asked questions I didn't want to think about. "What will happen when you have kids? You'll have to drive them around every day," she would say.

"I could move to a city," I said. "Lots of people there don't drive." I can't remember her response to that.

The worst ride home was from a night class in graduate school from a classmate's boyfriend who was stonily quiet. There were many times I couldn't get rides to things like birthday celebrations at bars on the weekend because it was too unpredictable as to how I'd get home. This was pre-Uber. Nick traveled a lot for his job, and sometimes I was too shy to ask a friend, or just didn't feel like it. I got to know friends' cars so well, ones with no air conditioning and rearview mirrors decorated with leis.

The accident could have been so much worse. I was t-boned at an intersection, but didn't get a scratch, nor did the other person. My car was totaled, but I got a new one. So what? People get in accidents all the time much worse than that and drive again the next day. What was my problem? Nick gave me rides to school, and he always drove when we went anywhere, so maybe that was part of the problem. I didn't have to immerse myself in getting over my fear of driving because I had Nick to help me, so I didn't. That was probably a mistake.

Through practice, very early in the morning before anybody was on the roads, I was able to drive slowly to my school's parking lot and the gas station. Time passed. I had one baby, then another one, and I drove them around our town. But I never got on the highway, and I only drove when it couldn't be avoided. I was always aware of my fragility.

I got a new job, and it was in a neighboring city. I looked online at Rideshare for carpool options. Anyone could place an advertisement, saying what they needed. Most people had to get to work, others, something else:

"Needing a ride to Utah or NV at the end of July," or "Headed down to Louisiana at the end of July. Looking for a ride along." or "A ride to go to Cali," and one alarming, "Ladies, need to get out of town?"

Some people had very detailed entries, and stated their best qualities, type of humor, and romantic situation—"In a carpool, I'm a good listener! My sense of humor is campy/cheesy! I'm single!"

Some were very brief: "I sleepwalk and am unable to drive for the next 6 months."

I just couldn't do it. Instead, I asked the receptionist at my new school if anyone else at the school carpooled, and she got the name of a social work professor who lived in my town.

Our pick-up spot was a parking lot of a call center close to my house. I would always arrive early so I could jump in her car with my messenger bag and canvas lunchbox, causing her as little inconvenience as possible. On the first day, the social work professor told me about her Weight Watchers meetings. She had a metal to-go cup of flavored coffee and a chocolate breakfast bar. A few days in, she said that although she barely knew me, she had a crisis going on and needed someone to talk to. It was quite a drama, complete with her boyfriend's ex-wife behaving badly, his son moving in with them, the legal system, the police, and the local news. It went on for weeks and weeks, and then months and months. It was all we talked about to and from work.

I tried once to drive on the highway. Nick's mom was visiting and watched our children. He and I got in my car, he in the passenger seat, and I drove us to the nearest on-ramp to the highway. I hated it. Everything was going too fast. "Is my car shaking?" I yelled to Nick over the noise. "No, you're doing fine," he said. "Try to relax." But I got off at the next exit, and that was it.

As the social work professor and I were driving home from work one evening, she was talking to her boyfriend on speakerphone. I sat silently, as I always did when they spoke on speakerphone. The boyfriend did not know about me. This was during the time when the police were getting involved in the scandal with his ex. He said to the professor, "This is the worst day of my life."

We ended up moving so I wouldn't have to carpool anymore. At least that's the answer I tell people when they asked why we moved. And that's what I tell myself. But what does that mean? The issue is far from resolved. I drive myself and the kids all over our town, even during the busy times of the day. I break the rules on websites about safe driving: I listen to the radio and sip drinks, I even snack. But I know I could be relegated to passenger stance easily. I came close just the other day, driving my daughter to a ballet lesson. I sideswiped a car and bent my side mirror. I thought about stopping, but knew that the car owner would look at my un-matching eyes and paralyzed face, and I was afraid of what they would say. Would they say I shouldn't be driving? What if they were right?

When I told Nick about it that night, he drove by the other car, parked in front of a house a few streets down, wanting to see if there was any damage. When he came through the back door, I was anxiously waiting in the kitchen. "Police everywhere," he said. "What did you do?" Then, "Just kidding."

Now

I don't hear back from the surgeon for weeks. When I do, it's a form email, saying that if I'd like a consultation, I need to make an appointment. I softly shut my laptop.

How to Look

Every pick-up and every drop-off, I looked for the two Barbie Moms. They wore these incredible outfits that could be titled things like Country Club Lunch (black and white bouclé jacket, jeans, heels, and pearls), Workout with Antonio (leggings, hot pink sneakers, and a white tunic), and of course, Garden Party: (jungle print flouncy dress and cork high-heeled wedges.)

Lunch Downtown with the Husband (wine ponte sheath), Tennis Practice with the Girls (white pleated skirt, sleeveless white polo, white visor, and sneakers), Silent Auction Planning Meeting (cream quilted car coat, navy pans and cognac driving moccasins).

I could never understand how they got their hair to look so shiny, so curled, so full. It reminded me of the commercials for spray-on hair for men. Their faces looked sprayed on, really, but in a well-done way.

Every few months or so, I remembered to check out a social media feed of a childhood friend who is now famous on the Internet. When we were kids, the friend said her father was the agent for Joey from *Full House*. Her father had divorced her mother, moved to California, and the friend and her siblings stayed with the mother in Michigan. Sometime after high school the friend moved to L.A. and got married. Now she was an impossibly beautiful influencer and mogul with a baby, who wore things like floppy felt hats, crop-top sweaters, and high-waisted jeans that highlighted sculpted abs. She also posted fitness videos of herself doing crunches and leg lifts while her baby ran around in his diaper.

There she was in a black sports bra and leggings, doing crunches while her towheaded child looked on, or in the same outfit but in olive green, executing lunges on a sidewalk while simultaneously pushing him in a stroller. In the background, there was a lush lawn and palm trees, and in the corner a two-story white house with tall windows. Her captions said things like "Grateful for the journey that led me here" and "Workout with my babe gotta get it in somehow!" Hundreds of comments followed each photo, such as, "Bodygoalz#" or "Your husband is a lucky man!"

When I looked at these photos, I felt not-great about myself, which was why I didn't do it too often. But I couldn't stop completely. I could be in my car, enjoying a few more moments of being sedentary before going into a coffee shop, say, or my office, taking a break from checking email, but I tapped my phone and entered another world, thinking it would be, what exactly, entertaining? My own life, in which I usually was content, looked chubby, tired, and financially-strapped in comparison to this former friend's.

*

There was always something wrong with my own outfits, never mind my makeup and hair. Mine weren't outfits so much as pieces of clothing paired together over and over again—even when I bought something new it looked like something I already had. Jeans that were baggy in some places and too-tight in others, scuffed boots, and oatmeal sweaters. Any makeup I put on looked strange—the eyeshadow looked too bright, and I blotted the lipstick until it disappeared completely.

Mimosa Mixer: (Gingham popover, white jeans and espadrilles), School Volunteer Day (Polka-dot button down, jeans, and red leather sneakers).

I had the feeling I had to get professional help to look like the Barbie Moms. I had gone to a cosmetics counter in a department store once, years ago. I remembered being surprised at the amount of products the makeup lady used on my eyes alone: a specific concealer for under them that was thick like spackle, another yellow cream for the lids, and a pencil highlighter for the inner eyes. And that didn't even include the shadow and liner. I had spent a lot of money that day and walked out of the store with one little bag.

That time, all of this makeup was for a job interview. I remembered the feeling of wearing all the new makeup, waiting in line at a coffee shop before the interview in my pantsuit, holding a newspaper whose front page I had only skimmed, too distracted by how great I looked, how great I felt. Maybe that was the way the Barbie Moms felt all the time? How could they not?. Where were they coming from every day, looking so glamorous? Where was there to go in this small, Midwestern city?

Afternoon on the Boat (Raffia fedora, black-and-white striped T-shirt, khaki twill shorts, and loafers), Parent-Teacher Conferences (Tweed blazer, jeans, beige suede ankle boots).

I don't remember anything from that job interview—a flash of the pink and beige office, the view of the Southern California coastline as I'd driven home, only that I ended up getting the job. I was in a completely different career now, living in the Midwest, but the point was I had once been Barbie-like, for a day, but looking like that every day for years and years, as the Barbie Mms did, well, that was something else entirely.

Also, why did they do it? Was it what their husbands wanted? Did they want perfect-looking wives? I couldn't imagine what Nick would say if I turned up at home looking like they did. What if I placed a polished fingernail on his lips and gave him a kiss? What if I was wearing a dress in the middle of the week for no reason?

"Um, who are you?" he would say.

I found myself wondering other things about the Barbie Moms: for example, did they cook their families dinner? I was on a beans and rice kick, and I had learned a way to cook brown rice in the oven that made me feel smart. I couldn't imagine the Barbie Moms chopping onions or opening a can of beans. Of course, it could be possible that they had cooks. My realtor proudly had one, a woman who came a few days a week leaving salads, soups, and homemade bread. If my realtor had a cook, then the Barbie Moms probably did, too. But what else was different? What else did I do that they did not?

Well, for one, I got in an argument with Nick last night over a trash can I had bought.

"Why on earth would you buy that right now? We have a perfectly good one already" he had said, squinting at our bank balance on his computer.

I put down my book. "We just had a conversation the other night about how we both hated it. You said it was too small and I agreed. The lid is also a pain."

"I didn't mean go out and buy a new one. I could live my whole life with that trash can and be fine," Nick had said. Then I went upstairs to bed.

Louise, Simple Night at home (I blanked, I changed into my Radiate Love T-shirt and black flowy pants right after we cleaned up dinner), Dinner With Friends (Again, nothing. I had been wearing my stretchy jean shorts and Life Is Good shirt a lot lately).

By the way, Barbie Moms is a compliment, I wanted them to know, or at least more of a compliment than not. It's a name that implies you look like a Barbie: physically perfect, meaning impossibly so. Not a smudge, a sag, or a loose thread. Not real, but alive, somehow.

*

I showed my mom my old friend's feed. My mom was a realist who bought presents fully expecting the recipient to take them back. She doesn't believe in wrapping. "I'm a horrible gift-giver," she says with a shrug. "The receipt's in the bag." The two of us were out for a hike during a family vacation in Colorado. As we trudged up hills around a muddy meadow, my mom reminisced on this Instagram-celebrity woman's family and what has become of them. She knew them too, long ago.

"They're just beautiful people, and yes, they have a lot of money," my mom said, not winded at all by the fast clip. "Some people are like that. Luck and good genes. It happens."

I huffed, but kept up. "Well, maybe she's secretly unhappy. I mean, photographs don't tell the whole story. Maybe it's an empty life," I said.

My mom laughed. "I don't know, she looks pretty happy in the photos to me."

It was true. That day's photo featured the woman on a trip to New York City in Central Park, wearing a white furry short jacket and a quilted leather Chanel backpack. She held a paper cup of what I was sure was black coffee. I had been trying to drink black coffee for years, but kept going back to slipping in half-and-half.

I also felt guilty every time I looked at these photos because I shouldn't be wasting time anyway. I had a family and a job. A messy house. I thought about all the other chunks of time I had wasted looking at childhood friends' photos on social media, including:

· A former volleyball teammate who married a much older man, lived in one of the most expensive cities in the world, and traveled bi-monthly to run marathons. Currently, she was on a "Babymoon in Australia with my hubby." She had posted photos of herself trying on outfits in dressing rooms.

· A woman who had been in the popular crowd in high school. She lived in Florida, had breast implants, and gave updates about her dog.

· A neighbor who was a year older and gave me rides to school when she remembered. She smoked, and I wanted to be her. Now she lived in the mountains and had four kids and a husband, who does something lumberjack-like.

The list went on and on. It was endless, and fruitless, I knew. So I stopped looking, for a while. I felt better about myself. I noticed that looking came as naturally as breathing, it's a muscular-reflex, but that I stopped it, and phew, that was close. But then one day I remember the childhood friend, and my kids were too loud and running circles around the house, and my fingers, so quickly, found her. Today showed a photo of her living room decorated for the holidays, frosted: a silver tree, gold ornaments, a sparkling platinum garland on a white fireplace in an all-white house, I was sure. Who lived here? Not me. Most definitely not me.

How Not to Volunteer

Book fair: When I arrived at Olive's school, I spent a long time just shopping for books, because that's what I saw the other mom volunteers doing. Then, finally, the volunteer organizer showed me how to ring up a purchase. By then I had been there for nearly an hour, and I had signed up for three. The children started coming in, and I tried to help a few of them find the books they wanted, but they seemed like they didn't need much help, and I told the volunteer organizer I had to leave early because something came up at work. Then I drove through Dunkin' Donuts.

Daycare board member: Bruce's daycare needed eight parents to serve, and there was a forty-five dollar monthly bill reduction if you did it. But the meetings were long, at 5:30 p.m. once a month, and I never said anything. The board president was a lawyer, had a cartilage piercing, and drove a Hummer. After the meetings, when Nick asked me what we talked about at the meetings, I always shrugged irritably as I peeled plastic wrap off of a dinner plate he had saved for me in the fridge. The answer always amounted to "nothing, really," although the topics varied: The high rotation of quitting childcare workers, a broken drinking fountain, a licensing requirement of fresh pea gravel on the playground—there was always lots of need but very little money. At the yearly chili feed to raise funds for new playground equipment, I signed up to bring a pot of chili and then forgot to attend.

Move Crew: Each August, university faculty are supposed to help new students move into the dorms. I showed up at 8 a.m., wearing my assigned T shirt, looked around, and recognized no one. I found the volunteer coordinator and was told to just "find someone and help them move!" I watched as fraternity guys, also volunteers, carried microwaves and wooden crates filled with shoes up stairs, stepping two at a time. I left.

Thanksgiving Feast: It turned out that parents were supposed to bring a food made with pumpkin for the children to try, as we all sat at a lunch table in the cafeteria. I hadn't brought squat. I had, really, seen the title "Thanksgiving Feast" in the class newsletter and thought we would all be feasting. Some parents had brought kid-friendly things, like pumpkin muffins with butterscotch chips or pumpkin ice cream. Then there was someone who had brought a can of pumpkin, opened it, and stuck a spoon in there. No kid tried that. I ended up joining the other parents and serving the kids, giving a few kids seconds of one dish or the other (mostly pumpkin-flavored marshmallows) and then hung back by the food table and ate loads of the pumpkin flan that one of my favorite moms, who had worn a Pearl Jam T-shirt the first day of school, made from scratch.

Ballet performances: The first time, I was a dressing room chaperone, and we were in the bowels of the cavernous performing arts center. The chaperones' jobs were to change fourteen four year-olds into cherub angel costumes and then out again. The white robes hung on a rack with each girl's name on the hanger. One woman took charge by yelling out each girl's name by hanger and had great running commentary. The other woman had her toddler twin boys along and was no help at all. I had never been so desperate as when I tried to get a girl's street clothes back on her. The girl acted as if she'd never gotten dressed in her life.

The next performance I was assigned to stand by a door and open it if someone came up. I had a feeling that was because of my poor contribution in the dressing room with the cherub angels.

The next one, I herded the now five-year-olds from the basement to the stage and back again after their dance was over, and then made sure no one left for three hours, with access to neither food nor water. I ended up walking out with Olive at 9 p.m. because I couldn't take it anymore. For days afterward, I half-expected to get a call from the ballet police, yelling at me.

The final one was the recital, and I now had a clipboard. I was to make a check mark by each girl's name as they were dropped off by their parents. I had to sit by the girls and watch the first half of the recital from the rafters before they went onstage. One girl kept asking if her lipstick was still on. Another wanted her mother. Olive and I ate all the candy I had stashed in my purse, no one else wanted any. At the end, I forgot the clipboard in the dressing room so I couldn't make sure all the girls were picked up by their parents, but it looked that way because everyone else was gone.

Women's prison creative writing class: This one was the one volunteer duty I did that wasn't connected to my children, but for my teaching job. The women viewed me as comical, and played jokes on me. At our last class, the ladies (as I called them, not wanting to call them inmates, as that didn't sound very fun, and I wanted our class to be fun, but meaningful) had me read one woman's poem out loud because it had lots of profanity, and they laughed for a long time at how I read it in my "English-teacher voice" (their words). They hugged the other volunteer goodbye after every class, but they never hugged me. The other volunteer was a popular theater professor who always made great eye contact and asked me how I was with sincerity. She remembered every woman's name and gave them little back scratches. I never did things like that. I wanted to suggest that the women all fold pieces of paper in half and write their names on them, like makeshift nameplates, so I could keep everyone straight, but I never did.

For their end of the year graduation, (the inmates called it that but there was no credit earned, it wasn't a real course) we gave them gift bags filled with items that had been mostly donated: leather journals, colored pens, some chocolate candies. That was fun because it made the ladies happy. I was beginning to see that some kinds of volunteering I liked. Mainly, volunteering that necessitated buying things, like the doughnuts and fruit that the women had wanted as their refreshment at the ceremony. I had ended up buying croissants instead because the store was out of doughnuts, and had been afraid that the women would be disappointed. I also hadn't been sure of what kind of fruit to buy, so I bought bunches of bananas, clementines, and apples. I had brought way more food than I thought they needed, but the women ate it all.

More and more, Nick got frustrated with me when I volunteered because I complained about it so much. "Just don't do it anymore," he said. "Someone else will." Then a friend told me about this woman who paid a babysitter to take her daughter to Girl Scout meetings. "She's kind of my new hero," my friend said. I thought so, too. But that was a little wacky, right? We were at a city pool with our children when we had this conversation, lounging in the shallow end while our kids ventured deep, and the sun had just gone down. I had been trying to take my kids to the pool as much as possible that summer so they would become stronger swimmers. I wanted them to have every advantage

How to Have Double Vision

Seeing double indicates that something is wrong, but what if that something is permanent? Does that make it less serious? I think so.

*

All Olive and Bruce really know about my double vision is that I wear tape over the left lens of my glasses when I drive to make it go away. When one of Olive's friends asked about the tape on our way to a Girl Scout meeting, Olive said, "She had brain surgery, O.K.?"

*

My stepfather is a doctor, which means that I can call him with medical questions, mainly about my kids. I call in the middle of the night when my son's asthmatic cough turns into a seal's bark. Years ago, when I had my surgery to try to make the paralyzed half of my face move, and it was a much harder recovery than my mom and I expected, and he was the one who put on the surgical rubber gloves, filled a bowl with soap and hot water, and gently scrubbed crusted blood off my neck.

*

My depth perception is not very good. I always prep the coffee pot for the next morning before going to bed, and the other night I had the sink on, filling up the pot as I put a filter in the basket, and it was almost a minute before I realized the stream of water was about two inches off. Nick and I had a good laugh about it.

*

Double vision is why we own a giant T.V. It is the first thing people see when they come in our house because the living room is right off the entryway. I got it for $125 at a garage sale and it is bulky, not one of those new flat-screens. I love it. Coming over for the first time, a friend says, "This doesn't really seem like you," and gestures to the T.V. I felt like saying, "Well, I guess you don't know me," but it's not his fault.

*

I hate optometrist appointments. I need glasses because of regular near-sightedness, but when I go through the motions of the eye exams and they find out about the double vision, they always say, "We can't help you in that regard," and I always tear up, even though I didn't expect anything.

*

I love my new ophthalmologist. He tells me exactly what to do to stop my peeling cornea from getting worse. Because I can't blink my left eye, it dries out. "Sands of Sahara in there," he says, looking in through his machine. He tells me to put eye drops in every hour, to put another kind in four times a day, and to put another kind in at bedtime. He shoos the nurse who is typing these instructions away and does it himself.

*

I go back to see the new ophthalmologist after two weeks. He tells me my eyes are much better, to keep putting the drops in every hour, and to come back and see him in one year. "Once winter comes and the air is drier, you might consider sleeping with swim goggles on," he says. "That sounds uncomfortable," I say. He shrugs.

*

I realize I always fall a little in love with new doctors.

*

The new ophthalmologist escaped Iran as a teenager and emigrated to the United States alone, then later reunited with his parents. They now live in a town four hours away, and he drives to see them every weekend. I know all this from a framed newspaper article I read on the waiting room wall. In person, he mentions several times that he lives alone with his dogs and has taken to sleeping on the couch to try and correct sleeping on his stomach.

*

A friend, who sees the same ophthalmologist, tells me that the doctor flies to give a cousin in Paris a prescription medication he can only get in the U.S. "He literally gets on a plane, flies eight hours, gets off, has lunch with his cousin to give him the pills, and then flies home."

My friend tells me this while we are standing in my kitchen, as we often do, while our children are upstairs playing/fighting. She lives a few blocks away—we have alcoholic seltzer drinks in our hands, and we spend time taking mild jabs at our husbands and talking about nothing. This is to say that I have a good life.

Now

I start seeing a new therapist, and tell her everything, the emailing of the ex, all of it. She is soft-spoken, with a enormous office—two large chairs and a couch. I'm already using the box of tissues profusely. I settle in easily, I guess. We decide to tackle the weirdness, or maybe not so much, of contacting the ex.

"It seems to me that you sent the email show your ex that you are doing fine, but you're not," she says. "You're hurting. Why did you want to let him off the hook?"

I shake my head. I leave her office, stumped, and think about her question for weeks, on and off. Is it letting someone off the hook if they were never really on the hook to begin with, at least according to them? Or, is our self-image so powerful that I wanted to see myself as likable and friendly? Why?

How I'm Learning to Accept Myself as a "Frequent Faller"

I'm a "frequent faller." I hate it. I have reduced balance, one of the aftereffects from the brain surgeries. Because the doctors had to go into the pons, the center of the brain where things like breathing, swallowing, and equilibrium are controlled, they had to lift up the cerebellum, the part of the brain that controls, among other things, coordination, precision, and accurate timing.

Messing with those two parts of the brain has far-reaching effects as far as moving about is concerned. In the past, I could just be standing still, talking to someone, and suddenly tip sideways, as if on a ship. I would walk from room to room of my house clinging to walls. Now it's much better, but I always need a railing going up or down stairs, and doing things like walking and talking simultaneously can take a lot of concentration.

One fall this past summer was on the stairs on the way to Bruce's daycare. The stairs are concrete, and nothing is so hard as concrete when you slam on it. I feel embarrassed to say I was carrying my son, and when I fell on the stairs I also dropped him. Not far, he wasn't hurt, but he was crying. I had scrapes on my knees and elbows for weeks. The knees I could cover up, but the ones on the elbows kept peeking out from sleeves and under bandages. When someone would ask what happened, sometimes I told the truth, but sometimes, inexplicably, I made up something. I'd say I fell somewhere else, doing something else. I don't know why. Why would that sound any better?

Is it the shoes? Sometimes I want to blame it on my shoes—sandals. Birkenstocks. Maybe they are too loose on me, and catch in that place between the toes and the shoe. But then I remember that just two weeks ago, I fell wearing my tennis shoes. I was wearing my new yoga pants and ripped them, and the blood from my scraped knee never came out.

Maybe it's because we moved to a new city. Really—after more than a decade of living in the same town where I knew the best routes to everywhere, I was now negotiating new territory, and I had to figure out the safest routes, with the most level ground and least potholes, by trial and error.

I always have scrapes and bruises on my arms and legs. I only actually bite it once or twice a month, but there are countless times each week when I misjudge, say, a doorway and slam a shoulder, or stumble and knock a hip around a sharp corner.

Of course, people don't understand. Why would they? My realtor jokingly asked my husband if he'd been beating me. It was hard to smile.

I have a nurse friend who talks about how angry nurses get when a patient gets out of bed when they shouldn't and falls. People do not like it when adults fall when it could be avoided. I have a personal trainer, and we do balance exercises like trying to walk forwards and backwards in a straight line, playing catch standing on balance balls, and standing on one foot for as long as possible. My trainer used to feel bad about my tears of frustration, apologizing over and over, but now he doesn't. When talking to others, I try not to ever bring up that I have a personal trainer, and this goes back to my embarrassment about falling, too.

Why do I hate to admit to having a trainer, to falling? It has something to do with not wanting to admit I'm different, but why should I worry about that? I'm 34 years old, what do I care? Maybe because walking and having balance should be so simple. It seems like something I should have control over. Not being able to balance makes me seem so incompetent in other areas of my life. What can I handle if I can't handle this?

I have two small children I can mother, although it may not always be pretty. It means having conversations with my daughter, a kindergartner, about why my balance is bad or my left eye doesn't move, and making peace with questioning looks from parents in the pick-up line. I have a husband who loves me fiercely, even though I struggle at times with the image the world sees of a "normal" man with a different-looking woman. I'm also a professor, a job I love and cherish. To me, teaching is about connecting with students, and I love nothing more than having those moments in the classroom that leave me feeling reset and centered—I have found that feeling nowhere else.

I can handle life, even though it appears otherwise at times. Maybe I'm afraid that when I fall, I have lost my ability to be someone whom others understand, to play a part in the world, to relate to others. I need to remember that being different isn't the problem—feeling different is. Feelings are valid and should not be ignored, but I need to remember to look out, look around me, and take stock of all I have handled that is far more complex than walking a straight line.

Now

"Maybe," my therapist says, "Your interest in your ex is that he knew you one way, and Nick knows you another way. Maybe you're thinking about how it felt to be the old you."

How to Be a Midwesterner: In Three Acts

Act I

The hairstylist hadn't asked before he cut me the bangs. They were very short—two inches at most. After he did it, I said, "Oh!" and he said, "I thought it would look cute."

The first time he cut my hair, he had marveled at its denseness, but then said, "How am I supposed to cut this?"

He rented a place on a farm, and his cabin had no plumbing or electricity—on purpose. To wash dishes, he lit a Bunsen burner and heated water that he lugged from a pump outside in a kettle. He had told me living off the grid was connected to his experience of Y2K when everyone thought the world was going to end.

Later, I was not surprised to hear about his firing from the salon due to drinking and tardiness. I had cried at home about my unwanted bangs, but had not complained to the salon, I wasn't sure why. When I first met the hairstylist he had been clean shaven, but each subsequent appointment he had more and more of a beard, until he resembled a younger, red-haired Santa Claus.

The whole reason I had started going to him in the first place was my usual hairstylist, Luci, was always booked solid, and if I had to cancel an appointment with her, which I often did because of work or childcare, I was out of luck. Luci was glamorous, had two pugs, and seemed to be always going to or coming from Las Vegas, where there were lots of hair shows. I loved to find out what Luci was eating lately, as she stayed away from entire food groups but still managed to never cook for herself. My last appointment, Luci had been into black coffee, kimchi, and blueberries. She also went to a personal trainer who was her frienemy.

When I had my most recent appointment with Luci I asked about him. Was he alright? Was he still living in that shack in the woods? What was he doing for work?

Act II

I was told I would have to make a speech. As Nick drove our little car toward Kansas City, I read what I had written over and over aloud. It wasn't long, on a half-sheet of paper. He told me how it sounded, when I was talking too fast. It was sticky summer, and we arrived at a street bathed in velvety shade, with stone houses bigger than any we had ever seen up close. The one's whose address was on our creamy invitation had bushes that were shaped into animals and employee parking.

Inside, we were handed name tags. Nick whispered that he saw a portrait of George Washington on the wall. The chandeliers were low enough to bite. Rooms on all sides, one with puckered-silk walls and sofas on claw legs; one with a Christmas tree and wrapped presents though it was July; one with a black-and-white tile floor and crystal picture frames showing different weddings. All the people were in the backyard, holding drinks. Once outside, we saw that the pool seemed strangely small and normal, a brown brick patio, a splintery swing set.

I saw the PR woman who had emailed—a pink and green skirt-suit and lots of lipstick, with a name tag too, which is how I knew who she was. We shook hands and she said, "You're so young!" I would speak at the end of the gift ceremony, she said. "But for now, explore! Have fun!" And she disappeared.

Nick and I met some people and ate a bunch of macaroons and oysters, but I didn't get to make my speech. The PR woman either forgot to introduce me or decided I wasn't right for the event. It was a fundraiser for a brain-injury charity that commemorated the dead daughter of the old man whose house it was. Though I had brain surgeries, maybe they weren't the right kind. The daughter, one of eleven children, had been shot twice in the head during a burglary twenty-five years ago when she was home from college for the weekend. We all watched as the old man was presented with a painted portrait of his daughter. Although he owned the house he didn't even live there, he used it for events and had a home a couple of streets over that was for real. He and his wife had divorced and the children had long grown up. They had lived in this home when they were younger, said a man who said he was one of the sons. When they had been kids, they had not been allowed in any of these rooms, they had a special playroom on the third floor, he said.

Nick told me this story on the drive home. I saw him talking to the man, blond and slight, like a jockey, but I was across the room refilling my water glass. I had gone into a bathroom to cry about my skipped speech, but had not cried much. Nick had waited for me outside the door, and then taken my hand. Together we walked to the dessert table and loaded up our plates with more macaroons, lava cakes, and sugar cookies iced with the number "25," the years since the old man's daughter had been dead.

Act III

At a Margaritaville in the Miami airport, it was 11 p.m., and I found a piece of metal in my chicken. I showed Nick, and he clenched his fork with resolve.

"You're going to have to say something," he said.

Or maybe he didn't say that. Nick was even more chicken shit about speaking up about food orders at restaurants than I was. He would never send anything back, not even if he got shrimp when he ordered a steak sandwich or diet instead of regular. So maybe I said it to him: "I'm going to have to say something." Who knows what his facial expression had been. Probably nothing, at that point. It had been a day in airports—we were coming back from a vacation in El Salvador, and had missed our connecting flight to Kansas City, so were getting ready to crash in the airport hotel. The kids were beyond exhausted, staring into space as they chewed fries.

When the server came around, we stopped goading our kids to finish their food, and I lifted up the metal piece that looked like a staple.

"I'm so sorry," the server said.

"That's O.K.," I said. "But I shouldn't pay for this meal, right?"

She held up our ticket. "I've already printed it off," she said.

"Oh," I said.

I started eating again because I was pretty hungry and desperate. I found a few more metal pieces after that.

"The cook must have been cleaning the grill with one of those metal brushes," Nick said.

"I guess so," I said.

Now

When I feel stuck, like I can't get over events that happened long ago, I think about what Chanel Miller, author of Know My Name *said. On a podcast, she advised listeners to take an art class, to create based on what they did that day. Her example was cleaning up dog pee each morning in her house. She drew comics about it, talking about her old foster dogs and how they had trouble controlling their bladders. That's what she was doing each day, and it was different than the day before, no matter how slightly. Tonight is my first art class, a mixed-media one taught by the only person I could find, a Christian artist who teaches homeschool Bible-themed classes. We'll see how it goes.*

How to Be a Legend: Filling Out My Daughter's Fourth-Grade Study Guide

  1. The Legend of Night Driving

I can drive hundreds of miles each night. I can go pick a friend up at the airport, or be the designated driver home from book club and drop everyone off. I can run across town to pick up Thai food at 9 p.m., or go to Manhattan and see a concert. I am confident, hands loose at ten and two. I can even eat a sandwich with one hand, change radio stations, and look directly at headlights in the opposite lane.

What part of the story could be make-believe?

After the sun sets, I cannot drive. I feel a little like Cinderella. The last time I drove at night, I felt like I was in a blurry circus of blinking, smeary lights, and I couldn't be sure where the lines on the road were. Even with glasses, my vision is not good. Now, if I have to do something at night, like teach a class, Nick will pick me up, our kids in the back seat in pajamas. Sometimes I cut it close, especially in autumn when nightfall comes so fast. Recently, I found myself with a car full of students, driving back from a field trip, and everybody on the road started turning on their lights. Gripping the wheel, I dropped the students off at their dorm and sped home.

What historical truth is there to this legend?

Lots of people can't see well when they drive at night, it's a thing. There's not a lot you can do about it, but searches on the internet try to prove otherwise. Supplements, mantras, breathing exercises, exposure therapy. Consulting an expert. "When your kids are teenagers, get them to drive you around, that's what I do!" said my eye doctor.

Who is the heroine and what great deed does she do?

There is Uber in Topeka, did you know?

  2. The Legend of The Walks

My two-hour walk is a morning ritual. I grow strong, with muscled arms, from vigorously pumping them, as if holding imaginary ski poles. The air is cool, crisp, and my nature bath leaves my soul calm. I don't need to listen to anything but my thoughts, one after another, sliding down from my brain to my spine, then evaporating away.

What part of the story could be make-believe?

     Wild, rabid dogs and slimy, bramble-covered gullies. Crazy people. My thoughts: "I wonder why it always smells like sulphur here?" "What to do about the decaying salad mix in the fridge…. Throw away or try to stomach for lunch?" "Isn't it ridiculous how Mom can still make me so mad in two seconds by suggesting I'm a tight-ass for my brother being late?" Getting almost poked in the eye by the same branch each day. Facts learned from podcasts that Nick listens to with no facial expression. "Did you know Dolly Parton has been married since 1966? Did you know laughter is most often used as a social lubricant? Did you know kids have six times the energy of adults?"

"Most people come back from walks in a better mood. You seem more agitated," he has said to me more than once.

What historical truth is there to this legend?

     I do go on a walk almost every morning, but not two hour ones. One hour, if I'm lucky. I see scary dogs sometimes, foxes, deer, stray cats, suspect squirrels, weird people. People who talk to me while my headphones are on. People who don't look at me. I do trip or slip and fall. I also go on lots of walks where absolutely nothing happens.

Who is the heroine and what great deed does she do?

One day just five minutes down the road from home, I slipped in mud, and walked back. I had ripped my leggings. I changed into some different pants and went out again.

    3. The Legend of My Daughter and Me

     There once was a mother and daughter who defied all tropes. They were not best friends or enemies. They were never competitive or resentful of each other. The mother never saw herself in her daughter and was afraid for the girl. The daughter never wished the mother was different, like her friend's mom, who let her friend "really go for it" in the kitchen and bake cakes, or who lived in a house where "nothing was old."

What part of the story could be make-believe?

Sometimes my daughter must find me annoying. Sometimes we are so alike it can't be real, like how we both cannot put anything 100% away (a towel crumpled and hanging off a shelf in the bathroom) or how we cry when we're tired. How can she forgive me so quickly after I yell at her, for the ten-thousandth time, not to leave her shoes in the bathroom?

What historical truth is there to this legend?

Memoirs and myths such as *Mommie Dearest, The Book of Ruth, Medea*, almost any woman you ask. Lots of daughters hate their mothers, lots of mothers ruin things with their daughters, entire genres have been built on mother/daughter problems. How do mothers and daughters even have a chance?

Who is the heroine and what great deed does she do?

Last night, at dinner, I was telling Olive about my school's most recent health challenge, in which you self-reported how many minutes you walked each week. If you walked more than 420 minutes a week, you got a free t-shirt. Olive asked what happened if someone lied and said they walked more minutes than they really did to get a t-shirt, and I said a person would have to be a psychopath to do something like that. Minutes later, she repeated "psychopath" and I laughed so hard I spit out my drink.

4. The Legend of Getting a Dog

My dog is my constant companion, running beside me (or speed-walking?) on a golden-leaved trail. It is a kind of dog that doesn't bark, and never jumps on people or has to use the bathroom in the middle of the night.

What part of the story could be make-believe?

The amount of times Nick and I discuss getting a dog, or rather, I threaten to bring home a dog, has got to be up there with the amount of times Olive discusses her dreams. I peruse breeder websites, look longingly at purposeful dog walkers out on the trail, and quiz dog owners, especially first-time ones.

What historical truth is there to this legend?

Last week I badgered my middle brother on Zoom

"So, what do you think? Would you recommend it?" I said. Nick rolled his eyes beside me. My brother sat with his four-year-old on his lap.

My brother's answer was not what I wanted.

Who is the heroine and what great deed does she do?

  I met another fourth-grade parent in front of our children's school to ask him about his dog, a $1,500 labradoodle. The dad had brought the dog so I could play with it, and it felt as soft and plush as a stuffed animal. The dog's name was Waffles, and as the dad held the dog's leash, my kids ignored it and tugged on my body to leave. "That's not really a great sign," the dad said.

  5. The Legend of the Neighborhood Email Listserv

  Once there was an email listserv so helpful, it was envied by those outside the area. Baking ingredients, gardening tools, newspapers—anything could be borrowed. Any question answered (How to prevent termites? Where is the fastest place to get a flu shot? Schedule of food trucks in the city?). Every morning when I woke up, the listserv emails were the first ones I opened.

What part of the story could be make-believe?

  My neighborhood has an email listserv that hosts many fights. It is owned and monitored by a longtime resident who keeps the server in his basement. It was damaged once when there was a flood, and the algorithms are such that half the emails end up in everyone's spam folder. Chuck, the owner, is a genius and a true renaissance man. When I have a question about knife sharpening, I write him, and receive a long email twenty minutes later full of links and tips on using a whetstone. He runs ultramarathons, and I have eaten his "chocolate pasta" he made one year for the neighborhood progressive dinner. It tasted like mushrooms.

What historical truth is there to this legend?

  The most recent email fracas was about Halloween and whether the neighborhood should host trick-or-treating because of COVID-19. Neighbors were calling each other by their last name, using the word "lynching," and citing the CDC.

There have also been email fights about fawns (two fawns roam the neighborhood and some worry about them getting hit by cars or fed human food, while others think they're cute, pet them, and post photos of them profusely); flag-stealing (four rainbow pride flags were stolen off a home's porch one summer, and one neighbor said it may just have been "troubled teen" and to relax); and missing packages.

Who is the heroine and what great deed does she do?

Some neighbors have unsubscribed from the listserv, and others simply never read them. To me, those are the heroines. Some, though they move across town or to another city or state, stay on the listserv.

My friend's parents moved out of the neighborhood and across town ten years ago, but her mom still follows the goings-on, and I chat with her about it all whenever I see her. I like the way she shakes her head and rolls her eyes at whatever drama is playing out in our inbox. She always says, "I'm so glad we're away from all that now."

A List of What I Did and Did Not Know About Facial Paralysis

What I did not know

     1. How much "loss" occurred in the definition of the word "paralysis." "Complete or partial loss of function in any part of the body. 2. Loss of the ability to move; or, 3. A state of powerlessness or inactivity."

What about loss of the ability to move on?

     2. I did not know facial paralysis starts in the brain. It occurs when cranial nerve number 7, also known as the facial nerve, is injured. Sometimes this is because of a stroke, where a supply of blood is reduced or blocked completely, depriving the brain of oxygen and nutrients. Sometimes injury to this nerve happens inadvertently during surgery. This was my case, because I had a malformed blood vessel in the pons that bled and needed to be removed.

     When I looked up images of cranial nerve 7 online, I saw how it and the other cranial nerves were plugged in like wires to the brainstem, and the pons was in the center. My brain looks like that, except for invisible damage. When the surgeon had to go remove the cavernous angioma (the malformed blood vessel that looked like a raspberry) from the pons, he had to move cranial nerve 7 aside, which it didn't like. It stopped working, partly.

     3. I did not know that I would ever want to try to fix the paralysis again, trying another surgery after 15 years. This new procedure is to try and restore movement to the paralyzed half of my face.

     A few months ago, I started following a couple of plastic surgeons on Instagram. I don't know why I did that. These Instagram accounts featured surgeons in Beverly Hills. A woman with partial facial paralysis a lot like mine popped up on my feed. She had a procedure where they took nerves from her ankle and transplanted them to the not-working side of her face. There, they grew and restored spontaneous movement. For example, if she were sitting in a dark room watching a movie and something funny happened, she would smile to herself unconsciously. A real smile, where both corners of the mouth moved up the same amount and showed an even row of top teeth.

That was what I wanted.

In the 10-second video, she blinked and smiled, silently. She was pretty, wearing eyeliner and mascara, and had freckles.

My smile happens when I press the tip of my tongue to the spot behind my top teeth. That's because a procedure in 2006 spliced a cranial nerve and joined it with a tongue muscle. But it doesn't happen fully, meaning the top corner of my mouth only moves a couple of millimeters, not enough to show teeth. Thus, all photos of me show me smiling with my mouth closed, giving a kind of Mona Lisa smile. It doesn't look awful, but my eyes never get pushed up and squinted like a real smile makes them. Also, it's not spontaneous, so if I hear something funny on the radio while I'm driving, my smile would just be my jagged, half-face one.

But a full smile just because I find something funny, like when I am sitting in a dark room watching a movie by myself? I could barely imagine it. But I could imagine it enough to want it.

4. I did not know that after seeing the Beverly Hills surgeon on my feed, I would go upstairs and woke Nick up. It was a Saturday morning, early, and both of the kids were still asleep. It's a little mean to disturb Nick's sleep, but sometimes when I was surfing the Internet in the early morning and found something exciting (an Air B & B availability that seems too good to be true or a stand-up comedian coming to our city) I would have to woke Nick up to tell him. This time, I crawled under the covers and tried to whisper as I told him about the Beverly Hills surgeon.

"What do you think? Should I email this guy guys? Schedule a consultation? I don't really want to have surgery out there, though." We had been through this a few months before with a surgeon in Houston. I had received no reply.

Nick had his eyes closed and cleared his throat. He was shooting a wedding until late the night before, but even if that hadn't been the case, he was a champion sleeper and could still go back to sleep after this if I let him. Which I would.

"Why don't you ask Dr. K, the one who did your last one? See if this is legit or not," he mumbled, and turned on his side.

"Oh, great idea," I said, and hurried off.

I emailed my former surgeon at the Kansas City hospital. Rather, I emailed his office, and a nurse wrote back the next day. "Dr. K says hi!" she wrote. She directed me to a new surgeon who was trained in this nerve transplant procedure and a specialist in facial paralysis. There was an open slot for a consultation in two days. I took it, and filled Nick in that night. He nodded slowly and held my hand. "Of course we'll go," he said.

Dr. Flynn was young and handsome, with dark hair. Thin. When I made jokes during our appointment, he looked down and smiled instead of laughed. I Googled him later and found some marketing photo for the hospital. He was backlit by powerful operating room lights, wearing a surgeon's cap, mask and blue scrubs. He looked steamily at the camera. When I went back the next day for the photo again, I couldn't find it, no matter how much I searched.

When I typed "dr" into Google, I got, "Dr. Fauci," "Dr. Dre," "Dr. Strange," then "Dr. Oz."

5. I did not know how the surgeries would work

It turned out that there were two kinds of procedures I could have: the one I saw on Instagram, the ankle nerves, spontaneous smile one, and then one with a higher success rate, which involved taking a "snip" of a muscle from the thigh and splicing it with one of the three chewing muscles (you don't need all three, the internet says) so that when I bite down, I will smile. But it's not spontaneous.

"If you were six years old, the ankle one would be more likely to work," Dr. Flynn said, perched on a stool across from me at our first consultation. Nick took notes on a memo pad. I looked into Dr. Flynn's eyes, and he looked back, steadily. "But as we get older, our nerve growth slows down. Sometimes nerves completely stop growing. We don't know why."

On the drive home, Nick took my hand. "Wasn't that appointment good news?" he said, speeding back to Topeka so he could be at a photo shoot on time and I could go to my Lunch Break Pilates class. "You have choices, options. We never knew!"

I shrugged, didn't say much. I wanted more of a sure thing. The "Befores" and "Afters" on Instagram didn't say anything about the procedures' success rates. I had forgotten about all of that, that chance of nothing happening at all, or worse, being worse than when you started. But by that evening, I wrote the nurse, Kasey, on MyChart and said that I wanted to do the chewing-muscle surgery. After the kids were in bed that night, Nick asked, "Won't you always wonder?"

"I'll always wonder about a lot of things," I said, but I didn't really know if that was true. Two weeks later I changed my mind and opted for the ankle one. The desire for spontaneity was too tempting.

What I did know about facial paralysis:

1. It destroys your confidence. After my facial paralysis, I didn't smile in pictures for a long time. Years. I still only do a closed-mouth smile, nothing with teeth or too wide, in which the paralysis would show too much. I didn't wear any jewelry, wanting to draw no attention to myself. I started looking at the floor when I talked to anyone I didn't know really well.

When I investigated the Beverly Hills surgeon, I scrolled through "Before" and "After" shots of some other patients. In the "Befores," they looked pretty grotesque, almost fake, grinning as wide as they can on one side of their face and then the other half as if it were made out of stone, or even worse, heavy, wet, clay, sagging. I thought "Oh my god, these people look horrible," and then a second later, "That's what I look like." Then, "How can I have gone around looking like that for so long?" and then, "But I did. I do."

The paralyzed half of my face doesn't sag, and even has what Dr. Flynn calls "tone," thanks to earlier surgeries like the tongue/teeth one. I am relieved I did those.

2. I did know that Bell's Palsy is the most common reason for facial paralysis. Everyone knows this. Justin Beiber had it. George Clooney. Pierce Brosnan. Truck drivers get it from the wind from the highway blowing on one-half of their face, or so I have heard. For Bells Palsy, partial facial paralysis occurs because the facial nerve becomes inflamed. It's temporary, and can go away in weeks or months. "Temporary" is everything. "Temporary" closes my heart.

3. I did know that distraction would help me forget my preoccupation with the surgery, but only for a little bit.

I started to take a drawing class on Monday nights. On one of the many podcasts I listened to on my daily walks, a writer had talked about how an art class helped her feel less depressed. Less stuck. "You realize that every day is slightly different, that every day you can make a new drawing of something that happened today that didn't happen yesterday," she said to the interviewer. That sounded good to me. That morning, I had told Nick that it felt like time was not passing anymore.

The drawing class was held in a local artist's Christian studio/gallery, which was in a strip mall in between a drive-thru liquor store and a Laundromat. There were intense Biblical-themed paintings on all the walls—Jesus on a rock talking to a crowd with lightning in the background. Jesus looking up at the clouds with the sun shining through. Jesus wearing a crown of thorns, etc. etc.

The teacher was very nice, which made the Jesuses not matter so much. I sat next to a middle-school principal, and our task was to draw a stool on the table in front of us without looking down at our paper. We both did horribly and laughed about it. It felt great.

The next week, our task was to copy a professional drawing of a person, but upside down. When I tried the first time I ran out of room, and there was no space for the person's head on the bottom of my paper. No matter.

4. I did know that some people in healthcare are angels from heaven. Dr. Flynn's nurse, Kasey, talked to me like a sorority sister. I loved her for this immediately, the normalcy she brought to these appointments, which were anything but normal.

While we were waiting for Dr. Flynn to inject some Botox into my forehead, to even out the paralyzed side and the non-paralyzed side, she asked Nick and me what we were doing afterward. Dr. Flynn's office is in Kansas City, about an hour away from us, and close to fancy stores we don't have.

"I want to go to Trader Joe's, but I'm not sure Nick's on board," I said, looking at Nick, and he shook his head and smiled.

"Kasey, she just buys a bunch of chocolate-covered stuff we don't need," he said, half-heartedly.

Kasey handed me an ice pack for my forehead, the hospital kind that you break in half in order to get it cold.

"Stop! Trader Joe's is the absolute best, you have to take her," she said, and we high five.

Dr. Flynn came in the small room and started to put the syringe together.

"We're talking about Trader Joe's," Kasey said.

"Ah. I'm an Aldi man myself," Dr. Flynn said, then told me to get ready and did three injections down the right side of the forehead.

"Oh, Nick loves Aldi. But I can't handle it: the quarter for the cart, the bagging from one cart to the other, it's too much," I said, and pressed the ice pack to my forehead. Even though the injections hurt, I would never have said so. My reward was when Dr. Flynn said, "Wow, most people think Botox really hurts." That was high praise for me.

We set a date for the big paralysis surgery a few months out, then got ready to leave. "Sooner or later, everyone's going to be an Aldi shopper," Dr. Flynn said, then shook my hand and left.

5. I did know that caring about facial paralysis comes and goes. Mostly comes. There are hours where I don't remember. Not days, though. And maybe not even hours, because even if I am laughing with my children, I am thinking about how I look laughing and hold a hand in front of my mouth.

Grading papers early one morning, in the old armchair and under a blanket, I read, "The moral of this story is that people will fall over and over again." At first I thought the student meant "fail over and over again." But either was apt. I don't think I am failing at life, or failing myself, exactly. But I know that I am failing to be content with what is. I am failing not to wish I were different. That is a recipe for disaster, to be sure. My hope is that each time I fail, or fall, it gets softer and gentler each time.

Epilogue

The pieces in this book were written during a period of years in which I was sometimes struggling, as we all do. Did writing this book change me? Absolutely. Many of the pieces in this book are about self-image through the lens of comparison, looking back, and wanting what is gone. I am in a different phase of life now, and I hesitate to say I am more '"at peace" with the way things are now (that seems to be inviting a crisis) but maybe I am. One thing is for sure: we have to wrestle with problems on our own clock, no matter how it might look to the rest of the world. I hope the pieces in this book demonstrate that.

Thank you to Nick, Olive, and Bruce for believing in me and in this book. It is because of you that it exists. Thank you to all at Finishing Line Press for bringing it into the world, especially Mimi David and Christen Kincaid. Thank you to my writing group: Jennifer Pacioianu, Karen Barron, and Raylene Penner. This book wouldn't be here without each of you, and I am so grateful for your careful reading, support, and friendship. I treasure it more than you know. Thank you to Caryn Mirriam Goldberg—without your careful reading and conversations this book would not have shaped up the way it did. Thank you for helping me see what this book could be during the earliest days of its creation. Thanks to my Washburn colleagues for listening to bits and pieces of this book at various readings and events. Your support (and laughter, if I could get it) was invaluable. Especially thanks to Andy Farkas, who read some of the earliest pieces. Thanks to Lindsay Metcalf and Corie Dugas for your guidance, support, and help in this world. Finally, thanks to my family on all sides for their support and interest in this book and this strange, wild world of writing.

Louise Krug's debut memoir *Louise: Amended* received a starred review from *Publishers Weekly* and was reviewed by Mary Karr as a "must read." It was also named one of the Top 20 Nonfiction Books of the Year by Publishers Weekly in 2012.

Her second book, a memoir-in-essays, *Tilted: The Post-Brain Surgery Journals*, won the Hefner-Heitz Kansas Book Award in 2018. Her work has been featured in anthologies such as *Dumped: Women Unfriending Women* and *Flash Nonfiction Food*. She is an Associate Professor of English at Washburn University in Topeka, Kansas, where she teaches creative writing and composition. She earned her Ph.D. and M.F.A. at The University of Kansas, and grew up in Holland, Michigan. This is her third book.

www.ingramcontent.com/pod-product-compliance
Lightning Source LLC
Chambersburg PA
CBHW020340170426
43200CB00006B/439